Mr. Fothergill's

GROWING
FROM SEED

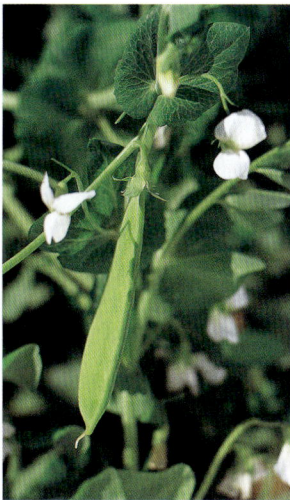

Margaret Hanks

MURDOCH
B O O K S

Contents

'Polka Dot' cornflowers in rich jewel-like colours

Planting
from seed

Since humans first
settled in communities,
seeds have been the
basis of life. The
earliest gardeners sowed the
seeds of wild plants, and after
gathering their crops saved some
of the resulting seed for sowing
the following season. As time
went on farmers selected only
the best of these wild strains for
sowing, and in turn the seed of
the best strains of these cultivated
crops was collected and
saved. Both yield and quality
progressively improved as a result.

Advantages of using seed

We are still dependent on seed crops for
survival—all agricultural production
starts with seeds, and vegetable, grain
and cereal crops are grown from seed.
On another, more personal level, raising
plants from seed is a thrill for the home
gardener. All gardeners find it very
satisfying to see something as small as a
pinhead emerge into a lovely flowering
plant or something good to eat. Nothing
beats the taste of fresh produce from the
garden or the delight of seeing a floral
display you've grown from seed.

Growing plants from seed is also
economical. If you are starting a new
garden or have large areas to plant out
with annuals, growing your own from
seed will save you a great deal of money.
If you are growing vegetables, you can
plant a few seeds at a time over a period
of several weeks to ensure a long
cropping period. This makes more sense
than having, say, ten lettuces or ten
cauliflowers ready for harvest at the same
time, which is what will happen if you
plant established seedlings. It makes
good sense and is good economy to
tailor your planting and, therefore, your
harvesting to suit your own particular
household needs.

Growing plants from seed is often the
only way that you can obtain a range of
unusual plants for the garden. Seed
companies produce a very large range of
seeds for annual and perennial plants that
are not available as seedlings or ready-
grown plants. The seeds often include
unusual colour ranges or unusual forms of
familiar plants. The less common types
of vegetables must also be grown from
seed. Quite a number of these vegetables
are best sown where they are to grow as
they will suffer considerable setback to
their growth if they are transplanted.
Seedlings of plants that you have sown
directly in their final position won't suffer

any root disturbance, and they won't require any interim period of re-establishment or hardening off. Direct sowing is easy with large seeds, and you can sow fine seeds in drills and pull out the excess seedlings to allow enough space for the plants to develop properly.

You can grow most plants from seed, although there are some that never set viable seed.

• Some plants with double flowers are sterile, as extra petals have taken the place of the reproductive parts. Formal double camellias, large incurved florists' chrysanthemums and exhibition dahlias are some of the plants that produce no seed and therefore have to be propagated by vegetative means. This means they must be grown from cuttings, division, layering, budding or grafting.

• Some cultivated varieties of plants must be grown by vegetative means to ensure the purity of the stock. These plants include named varieties of daylilies, shasta daisies, roses and citrus, as well as plants with variegated foliage.

Hybrids

You will find some plants always come true from seed while others may show variations. First generation hybrids of plants maintain the characteristics of the initial breeding, but if seed from those plants is saved and sown the following season the plants are likely to be different from the first crop. Seed companies ensure purity of these strains by exactly repeating those first hybrid crosses.

In nature and in the garden there can be seedling variation. This is the result of open pollination, where pollen from one plant is transferred to another by insects or by the wind. Plants grown from seed sometimes throw up something different or special, such as a colour variation, or variation in form or vigour. Plant breeders are always on the lookout for these

variations, which can be the source of interesting future stock. Most of the seed offered for sale by companies is open pollinated. The plants from which the seed is harvested have been grown in the open and pollen has been transferred at random from one plant to another (cross-pollination). Seed producers take care to separate blocks of plants where cross-pollination may be undesirable. However, cross-pollination is also the means of producing new strains of plants.

The first hybrid plants arose by chance; that is, they developed from plants that had cross-pollinated by means of insects or the wind. Growers noticed plants distinctly different from the rest of the crop and saved the seed. By sowing and growing that saved seed they could

WHAT IS A HYBRID?

A hybrid is a naturally or artificially produced offspring of genetically distinct parents. Hybrids display new characteristics and are generally vigorous in growth. An F1 hybrid is a first generation hybrid—to produce it, selected parents are used for each batch or production cycle. F1 hybrid seed conforms to a known set of characteristics. To maintain the character of an F1 hybrid and produce seed true to type, the same combination of parents must be used every time. If the F1 generation plants are allowed to breed by open pollination from a range of different potential parents, then the seed saved from these plants will produce seedlings with a range of variations. This seed is known as an F2 generation as it is not true to the original F1 cross.

discover whether or not the next generation of seedlings would come true to the known parent plant. If plants came true from seed and had superior features, the strain would be continued. This is how natural hybrids developed. Later, humans intervened, transferring pollen from a plant with desirable features to another plant with a different desirable feature to create an artificial hybrid. If this hybrid was a better plant, the same cross would be created again and again to produce an F1 hybrid.

Getting started

Growing plants from seed is interesting and straightforward. Begin by sowing easy-to-handle seeds that are known for their reliable germination. Flowering annuals with large seeds, such as nasturtium, sweet pea and sunflower, are ideal for first timers. Other easy annual flowers include alyssum, cleome, cosmos, forget-me-not, nigella, Virginian stock and zinnia. As long as you plant them at the right time of year and follow a few basic rules you should produce some excellent results. Vegetables that are easy to handle include beans, capsicum, cucumber, melons, peas, pumpkin, silver beet, sweet corn, tomatoes and zucchini, but there are many others,too.

Children's gardens

Try to give children a patch of sunny ground where their plants are likely to grow successfully. Kids will quickly be put off gardening if they have to work in a shady corner where plants may not come up or will struggle if they do.

Start children off with plants that have large, easy-to-handle seed or those that germinate quickly. Nasturtiums and sunflowers are great favourites. Also try Virginian stock and radish—although the seed is small, these plants will germinate, grow and reach maturity quite rapidly.

CLIMATIC ZONES

The maps opposite are a guide to the major climatic zones of Australia and New Zealand, showing the zones referred to in this book (in particular in the Planting chart on pages 153–5). Areas that are generally not suitable for the plants described are left blank.

There will, however, be some variation of the climatic conditions within these major zones. Gardeners may alter the natural conditions, for example by providing shelter from hot sun or frost, or by installing watering systems. To see which plants will grow well in your garden, check your neighbours' gardens. Your local nursery can also advise you.

'Peach Melba' nasturtium

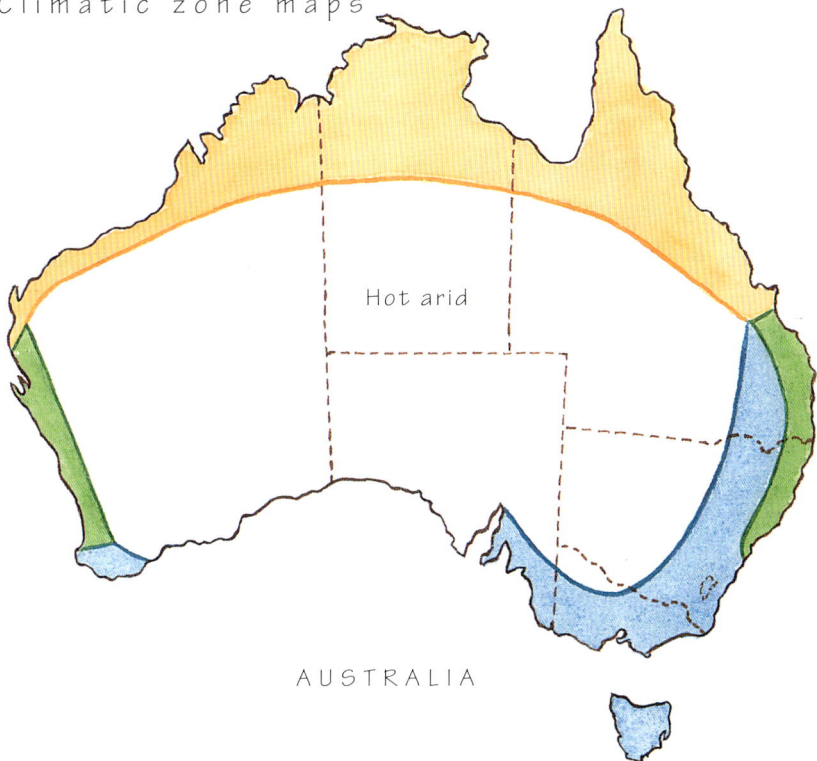

Climatic zone maps

Hot arid

AUSTRALIA

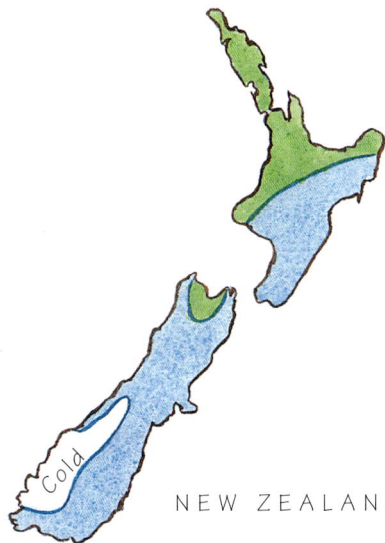

NEW ZEALAND

Tropical

Warm

Cool

How to
plant
seeds

Planting seeds is a simple process—as long as you follow a few basic guidelines you'll achieve a good success rate. You should be aware of the correct sowing times, as well as the correct sowing depth and spacings for your seeds. It is also important to follow certain standards of hygiene when you are sowing seeds in containers.

Once the seed has germinated, careful watering is necessary to achieve the best results.

When to sow seed

It is important for you to check seed packets for sowing times. The seed of some plants can be sown at almost any time of year but most seeds are dependent on temperature and/or day length for their germination and development. For a better chance of success you should follow the directions on the packet.

You should bear in mind that there can be considerable climatic variations from year to year which have a bearing on soil temperature and sowing times.

There are also variations in climate even within regions that might appear to be similar. For instance, spring may come early in coastal districts while only a relatively short way inland and certainly in high altitudes spring will come quite some time later. This particularly applies to soil temperatures. Do not to sow summer-growing crops too early in spring before the soil warms as this can produce disappointing results. In regions where occasional late frosts occur in spring, it is important not to sow seed of summer-growing plants outdoors until all danger of frost has passed. Sow seed in pots or trays and keep them in a warm frost-free place until it is safe to plant seedlings outdoors. When sown in the wrong season plants may grow reasonably well but fail to flower or set fruit. For example, sweet peas sown in warm zones in spring will grow but will not flower in high temperatures. Likewise tomatoes sown in autumn will grow and may even flower but they will not set fruit as the soil and air temperatures become cooler.

Depth and spacing

Seed packets also give details of suitable planting depth and spacing for that particular plant. Again, you'll find it is worth following the guidelines.

The rule of thumb is that seeds are planted at a depth of roughly twice the diameter of the seed. Fine seed is generally planted no more than 5 mm deep with a very light covering of soil or potting mix. Large seeds are planted deeper, according to their size. However, if you plant seeds too deeply they won't germinate and may rot in the soil.

Some seeds need light to germinate and should therefore not be covered at all. This information is indicated on the seed packet and is given in the individual plant entries in this book.

Good soil preparation prior to sowing is vitally important. If the soil is heavy and the drainage poor many seeds will fail to germinate.

Planting method

You can plant large easy-to-handle seeds at the appropriate spacings where they are to grow. Many large seeds are best sown directly into the ground or container where they will continue to grow without any need for you to transplant them.

Very fine seed is harder to sow, but you can still sow it where it is to grow and thin it out later to select the strongest plants at their ideal spacings. If you are having trouble sowing fine seed evenly without it all landing in one area, mix it with very fine sand to make it easier to spread the seed evenly. Some growers prefer to put the mixed seed and sand into a cone of firm paper or cardboard and then sprinkle the mix onto the growing medium. Using sand also shows where the seed has been sown, making it easier for you to firm it in and cover it. A salt shaker is also a very convenient tool for sowing fine seed. Alternatively, you can obtain proprietary seed sowers from nurseries.

If you are planting seeds directly into the garden you can make a furrow about 15 cm deep, sprinkle a little fertiliser into the base of the furrow and then refill it with soil almost to the original level of the ground. You can then sow your seed and firm down the soil surface. By using this method you can be sure that there is a ready supply of nutrients available for the developing plants, but there is no chance of burning the fine roots emerging from germinating seeds. This is the method most often used by vegetable growers, as vegetables must be grown rapidly in order to ensure the very best quality produce.

Boxes and trays for seed raising

If you are raising large numbers of seeds it is often most convenient to sow them into boxes or trays.

• In the past, seed boxes were always made of timber. Timber boxes are easy for the handyperson to build. They should be 8–10 cm deep with a width and length that make them convenient for you to lift and move around. The timber pieces that form the base of the box should be spaced slightly apart to allow for drainage.

• Plastic trays such as those used at nurseries to hold seedling punnets are ideal if you can get hold of some of them. You should line the base of the trays with a single sheet of newspaper to prevent the seed-raising mix from falling through the holes.

• Cell trays that hold individual seedlings can be purchased or recycled. These make transplanting very easy and are most suitable when you want to raise only a few plants at one time. You can also sow individual seeds in egg cartons— these can easily be pulled apart so that you can plant the seedlings without disturbing their roots. The cardboard carton will break down in the soil. You can cover your container of sown seed with a sheet of glass or clingfilm to help moisture retention; however, once seeds

An array of summer vegetables gathered fresh from the garden—all are easily raised from seed

have germinated remove this cover or the newly emerged seedlings may rot.

• Peat pots in which seeds can be sown are available commercially. Once the seedlings are large enough, plant them—still in the peat pot—in the garden.

• Ordinary plastic pots are also suitable for seed sowing, especially pots that are wide and squat. However, if you are raising tree seed you must plant the seeds in tall, narrow pots to avoid any setback of the developing taproot.

• Clean, used margarine or butter tubs are useful containers for seed sowing. Make sure that the tub will drain well by perforating the base with a skewer in several places.

• Seed-raising kits are also available, which provide you with everything you need to get started. In addition, you can purchase seed sowers and seed tape. These handy sowing kits are explained in more detail on the inside back cover.

When you are reusing pots or trays they must be scrupulously cleaned before you fill them with mix and sow the seed. If containers are not properly cleaned there is always the chance that the pot contains a residue of some soil-borne fungus or even insect eggs that may contaminate the clean seed-raising mix. Clean pots or trays by washing the pots thoroughly and disinfecting them with a 1 per cent solution of household bleach. You should stand the containers of sown seed on a layer of gravel, on bricks or on a weed control mat—never stand pots or trays directly on the ground as there is always a chance of introducing soil-borne pathogens via the drainage holes.

Sowing seed in containers allows you to get a head start on the following season's crop of flowers or vegetables. This way you can be assured of an almost continuous display of flowers and have vegetables ready to harvest early in the season. In districts with a short growing season, this is often the only practical solution. Check seed packets for the time that must elapse between sowing and flowering of annuals or between seed and sowing and harvest for vegetables. The higher temperature of the growing medium in the pot also helps germination. Another advantage is that you can move containers to catch the sun or take them under shelter to stop seed being washed away by torrential rain. You can keep containers away from snails that may destroy emerging seedlings and out of reach of digging cats or dogs. Those of you gardening in cool climates with a short growing season can sow seed in containers and keep them indoors on a sunny windowsill. When the danger of frost is over you can plant them out into the garden.

Cold frames and seedbeds

Even though few gardeners today use cold frames, except in cold climates, they are ideal structures for raising seeds. A cold frame is a raised enclosure, usually framed in brick or timber, with a glass or polythene cover. The frames are built higher at the back so that the cover slopes slightly, allowing rain to run off it. If the frame is being used mainly for seed raising it can be filled with a good seed-raising mix, and this large volume of soil or mix makes a cold frame much easier to manage than pots or trays. You will find there is less temperature fluctuation and fewer problems with the growing medium drying out.

You could also consider using a seedbed, which is essentially the same as a cold frame. A seedbed is a raised bed of convenient working size, probably no more than 1 m square, enclosed by brick or timber. A removable cover of 30 per cent shadecloth or flyscreen wire will provide light shading for seedlings and reduce the impact of heavy rain. The cover can either be attached to a metal or wooden frame with legs or it can be supported on bricks.

Watering

Once you have planted your seeds they must be kept moist until they germinate and emerge from the ground. After sowing the seed, water with a gentle, fine spray—you can use a hand spray mister or a watering can with a very fine rose, or you can turn your garden hose down to a fine mist.

If you have sown the seeds in pots or trays, stand the containers in water to allow moisture to percolate up through the mix without dislodging the seeds. Until the seedlings are growing strongly they should be watered very gently. You should water plants in the morning and then check them in the late afternoon, watering again if necessary. Seeds that are starting to germinate will be producing tiny roots under the ground long before you see any shoots emerge above the ground. If these tiny roots are broken or dislodged by heavy watering the plants will never have a chance to develop properly.

Although overwatering is one of the most common causes of failures with seed raising, it is also important that you check pots and containers every day to make sure they have not dried out too much. You should check them more than once daily in the summer months or in dry, windy weather.

If you have sown plants directly into the ground they will need less water, but you should still check them frequently. Some plants sown into well-prepared ground that has been watered heavily before sowing may not need watering again until seedlings emerge, unless the weather is exceptionally dry or windy or there is very low humidity. This is especially true in the case of peas, beans, broad beans and sweet peas, which will rot quite readily if you give them excess water before the seedlings emerge above the ground.

Types
of
seeds

A seed is made up of an embryo, a food storage structure to nourish the seedling during germination, and a protective covering or seed coat. All of the plant's genetic material is stored within the seed. Different seeds have different germination requirements regarding temperature, day length and exposure to light—although certain seeds will grow in almost any conditions.

Classification

Flowering plants are broadly classified into two groups according to whether they have one or two seed leaves (cotyledons). The monocots (monocotyledons) have one seed leaf and the dicots (dicotyledons) have two seed leaves. Monocots include palms, grasses, lilies, iris, freesia and sweet corn. Dicots encompass most flowering trees and shrubs, annual flowers and most vegetables—the majority of plants we know are dicots. They have two seed leaves, branched roots and either netted or reticulated veins on their leaves, and the flower parts are in multiples of five in many cases. Each of these two groups, monocots and dicots, has a range of characteristics that distinguishes it from the other.

Characteristics

The seed of a plant is contained within a fruit—which may not be anything like what we generally call fruits. These fruits are identified by names such as pod, capsule, nut, berry, drupe and follicle. Their size, shape and dispersal mechanisms vary enormously. Impatiens, for example, has an explosive mechanism. When the seed capsule is ripe, valves inside the capsule coil up and shoot the seeds into the air so that they are dispersed well away from the parent plant. Thistles and many plants in the daisy or Asteraceae family have silky hairs on top of the fruit, allowing seed to be carried long distances by wind; trees such as maple and ash carry their seeds in a winged structure where the wings behave like tiny propellors, again allowing seeds to be carried some distance away.

Seeds may be large like those of avocado or mango, medium sized like those of beans or sunflowers, or very fine like carrot, petunia or mustard seed.

Orchids have the finest seed of all: it is just like dust.

Viability

Seeds vary greatly, too, in their viability or ability to grow. Some have a very short period of viability while others may maintain their ability to grow over many years. Seeds from commercial growers have a use-by date on the packet which indicates how long the unopened packet should last in good condition and still give good germination rates. Fresh seed usually gives the best results, and after opening a packet it is advisable to use the remaining seed within six months.

Seeds must be stored in a cool, dry place, even in the refrigerator. Enclose packets of seed in zip-lock bags before storing them in the fridge. You can also store seed in the freezer for long periods. Commercially packaged seed is contained and sealed in airtight foil envelopes to ensure seed remains dry and clean.

High temperatures and damp conditions are the worst enemies of stored seed. In damp conditions seeds absorb moisture, providing ideal conditions for fungal organisms to take hold. If conditions are too wet the seeds may absorb enough moisture to swell and start to germinate; they will then rot, and the whole batch of seed will be lost.

Seed companies grow their own seed or contract special growers to produce their seeds to ensure that the packeted seed is of the highest quality. Their seeds are tested regularly for purity and germination rates.

Light requirements

Particular seeds have some very specific requirements regarding temperature, day length and amount of exposure to light, while other seeds can be grown in almost any conditions. Begonia and impatiens are examples of plants that need light to germinate—you should not cover these seeds after sowing. Other seeds you should not cover after sowing include primula and primrose, polyanthus and coleus. Mustard and cress will germinate on paper or cotton wool.

Different seeds for different climates

There can be a big difference in the growth and performance of plants grown from seed, depending on the source of the particular seed. Some plants may grow well in a range of different climates, but this is not always the case.

Seed sourced from plants originating in mild regions with light, free-draining soil may not perform well in areas that have heavy frosts or in areas with heavy clay soils, whereas seeds sourced from warm, low altitudes may not thrive in colder, high-altitude regions. Seed companies aim to supply seed that performs well in a range of climates, and they choose strains of seed with proven superior qualities.

Cool climate plants

Seeds of some plants are very sensitive to high temperatures and won't germinate if conditions are too warm. Lettuce, peas, spinach and primula are in this group.

Some cool climate plants will grow quite well in warm climates but will never flower, often because the lack of chilling prevents the development of flower buds. In nature, chilling stimulates growth and flowering in many species of plants. Seeds that mature in autumn sit in the ground (or in their containers), are dampened by rain, then chilled by frost or snow in winter, and finally burst into life in spring. Some seeds will not germinate unless they have had a sufficient period of chilling followed by a period of rising soil temperature and increasing day length.

GREGOR MENDEL AND HIS PEAS

Since the remarkable scientific observations and discoveries of the nineteenth century, more and more has been learned about plant breeding. Fundamental to this work were the discoveries of Gregor Mendel (1822–84), an abbot of the Augustinian order at Brno (in what is now the Czech Republic), where he taught natural history.

It is notable that Charles Darwin, in spite of his detailed experiments on inheritance in plants, did not discover the laws that are the basis of all modern genetics. This was left to Abbot Mendel, who in 1865 published the principles of the inheritance of characteristics in the garden pea.

When Mendel crossed a pure breeding tall plant with a pure breeding dwarf plant, all the progeny were tall. When these plants were self-pollinated, the next generation were approximately one-quarter dwarf and three-quarters tall. From this and other experiments Gregor Mendel deduced that the characteristics passed from parents to offspring were paired; only one of the pair came from each parent, and that one could be dominant over the other. When he dealt with two pairs of characteristics, for example tall or dwarf peas and round or wrinkled seeds, he found that they segregated and recombined independently and in predictable ratios.

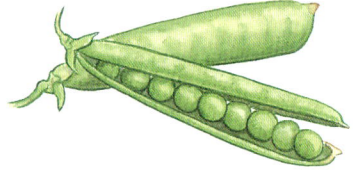

The importance of Abbot Mendel's work is that it showed there was no blending of the characteristics in the offspring. Mutations can be hidden as recessive characteristics in a population but are not diluted or lost. His work also showed that the recombining of 'factors' could give rise to plants with new characteristics. It is now known that Mendel's 'factors' are the genes carried by the chromosomes in the nucleus of the cell.

Mendel's work was not seriously examined until its rediscovery in 1900. Since then it has led to the modern science of plant breeding.

Warm climate plants

Plants that will not germinate in low temperatures include beans, eggplant and tomato. Grow warm climate plants in cool climates with the protection of a glasshouse, at least through the vulnerable stages of germination and establishment. Soil temperature is important for many summer flowering and cropping plants. Seed of these plants will simply not germinate if the soil is too cool. Cold soil can result in the failure of many summer annuals and vegetables if you sow seed too early in spring.

Vine-ripened 'Tropic' tomatoes

How seeds get into their packets

The varieties of vegetables and flowers in our packets come from both old and new strains. Some of the old varieties, such as the 'Queensland Blue' pumpkin, have been cultivated for well over 100 years. Other varieties are the result of more recent breeding programs; for example the 'Newmarket' carrot, which is a first generation (F1) hybrid.

Seed producers

There are very few seed companies that own their own seed-producing farms. Rather, they rely on farmers who grow the seed crop under contract. Seed companies such as Mr. Fothergill's are in close touch with leading seed producers and breeding companies throughout the world, and it is from this wide range of suppliers that seed stocks are drawn.

Seed producers who specialise in particular types of seed (for example that of petunias, which come in many different forms and in a wide colour range) must do more than simply offer the best strains they can and maintain these strains with a first-class breeding and quality-control program. They must also possess the techniques and the know-how and machinery to harvest their seed crops. Producers must be able to clean the seed lots to commercial standards, ensure vigour and high germination and also store seeds under ideal conditions.

A small quantity (often less than 50 grams) of 'elite' or breeders' seed is sown and grown by a contract grower as a crop, then the resulting crop is harvested to provide the 'mother' seed. This mother seed in turn is multiplied by several contract growers to produce the commercial seed that goes into our coloured packets.

Where cross-pollinated plants are being grown, the seed crop must be isolated by distance or time to prevent contamination by stray pollen from other varieties or closely related plants nearby. Unwanted plants in a seed crop, or 'rogues' as they are known, are removed prior to flowering and seed set.

Where is seed grown?

Seeds are harvested by professional seed companies the world over. Some countries tend to specialise in certain

Potted pansies and wallflowers

no rainfall are critical during the harvesting period—in less than ideal conditions the seeds may be damaged in the harvesting process.

The force needed to dislodge seeds from the plants may lead to mechanical damage and reduced viability, and can also result in high counts of 'abnormal' seedlings (that is, seedlings with insufficient root or shoot development). Although some injuries to seeds are internal and therefore unnoticeable, they may still result in unpredictable losses of germination at some time in the future.

Harvesting seeds that shatter

Another group of plants harvested for their seed are those that 'shatter' or split open to release the dry seeds, usually unevenly. This group includes delphinium, pansy, petunia, onion and cabbage. The plants must be harvested before they are fully mature, and are then dried or cured before the process of seed extraction occurs—as a result of this, some of the seeds will be underdeveloped and immature.

These plants are handled using the following processes:

• *Drying*. Plants are cut, sometimes by hand, or dry flowers and fruits are collected. They are placed on canvas or on a screen on the floor in a dry shed for 1–3 weeks. If only a few plants are involved they are often hung upside down in a paper bag to dry.

• *Extraction*. Commercial seeds may be harvested by special machines that extract the seed by gently beating, flailing or rolling the dry fruit. In addition to extracting the seeds from their fruit parts this process separates the seeds from dirt, sticks and other debris. By contrast, some plants need to be screened or rolled by hand. Lightweight seed, which is usually of no use, may be removed during this screening operation.

types of plant: pansies and violas in Holland; phlox in France; zinnias and marigold in the United States; petunias and cabbage in Japan; peas in New Zealand; beans, lettuce and sweet corn in Australia. Some crops like a particular climate and others don't. This tends to determine where seed crops are grown.

Harvesting field-grown crops

The professional seed producers who supply seed companies use a variety of techniques to harvest the large range of seeds. Field-grown crops such as corn, beans and sweet peas can be harvested using a 'combine', a machine that cuts and threshes the standing plant in a single operation. Plants that tend to fall over or are grown lying on the ground—such as sweet peas—are cut and piled, or windrowed, for drying and curing. Weather conditions of low humidity and

• *Seed cleaning.* This process may be required to eliminate all dirt and soil particles, debris, weed seeds and other unwanted seeds. Cleaning machines operate by means of a combination of shaking screens of various sizes, air flow and gravity separators.

Macerating vegetable seeds

A third group of plants harvested for seed are vegetables such as tomato, capsicum, eggplant, cucumber and pumpkin. These crops are grown over large areas and are picked when they are ripe—or even overripe. They are handled using the following processes:

• *Extraction.* For small lots, fruits may be cut open and the seeds scooped out and sifted through screens or washed in a fine wire basket. For larger lots, separation is carried out by fermentation, mechanical means or washing through screens. A macerator may be used to crush the fruits and mix the pulverised mass with water; this resulting mixture is then diverted into a tank.

• *Fermentation.* The macerated fruits are placed in large barrels and allowed to ferment for a period of about four days at 21°C, with occasional stirring. If the fermentation process goes on too long, the seeds may sprout. As the pulp releases the seeds, the heavy, sound seeds sink to the bottom of the barrel and the pulp remains on the surface. After collection, good seed is washed and dried either in the sun or in dehydrators.

Cleaning seed

Seed cleaning techniques are particularly interesting—a variety of methods and gadgets are used to achieve the clean seed that is offered for sale.

The raw, uncleaned seed delivered from the farm invariably contains impurities such as seeds of other crops, weed seeds, straw, insects, soil and dust.

All this is removed by machines that use a gentle combination of air flow, metal screens and wire screens to separate seeds from other materials of different weight, size, shape and width.

A machine called an indent cylinder separates seeds of different length, while a gravity separator is used to remove immature, shrivelled and damaged seed as well as soil particles.

Many other interesting and ingenious machines have been developed for the purpose of cleaning seeds. The velvet roll mill and the magnetic separator distinguish between seeds with smooth seed coats and those with rough coats. In a spiral separator, round seeds move faster than non-round seeds and are directed to a different outlet. A colour sorter uses a photo-electric cell to identify and separate varieties of seed with different coloured seed coats.

SEED QUALITY

Seed producers are constantly refining and improving techniques for seed harvesting, extraction and cleaning. Their ongoing work ensures that only the finest quality seed is being packaged for sale.

Gardeners who plant seed from packets can feel confident that as long as they follow the directions given on the seed packet excellent results should follow.

Of course it is also important for you to store packets of seeds correctly to achieve good-quality plants. The viability of seed will decrease with age, for example, and will decline rapidly once you have opened the packet. Seed should be stored in cool, dry constant conditions.

How seed germinates

To germinate, a seed must have ample water, a suitable temperature and be held in a well-aerated growing medium. Although most seeds require darkness in order to germinate, a number must be exposed to light. Information about specific germination requirements or any special treatment will be given on the seed packet.

The process

Once the seed is planted it absorbs water and swells. The seed coat may then break and the seed starts to respire (breathe). Uptake of water continues, the seed continues to respire and the seed's cell systems are activated to use the reserves of food stored in the seed. Cell division then begins and the root or radicle emerges. The seed leaf or leaves then push up through the surface of the growing medium. Sometimes the seed coat still adheres to the leaves, but it will fall off naturally in time.

Seeds absorb around 50 per cent of their own weight in water as they begin to germinate—therefore, if they dry out during this critical time they will lose their ability to grow. Seeds also require air as they begin the process of respiration, but if the growing medium is heavy or waterlogged there will not be sufficient air in the mix to sustain the growing seeds.

The mix must be at about the right temperature. Many seeds will germinate early to mid spring, when temperatures are usually 18–20°C. Some, however, prefer conditions to be cool and do well at about 15°C, while some summer annuals will germinate rapidly if temperatures are in the mid-twenties or above. If growing seed in pots or other containers, remember that the seed-raising mix in a container will be warmer or cooler than garden soil at a given time of year because of its small volume as well as its all-round exposure to the air.

The majority of seed germinates in darkness, that is, under a covering of soil or potting mix. There are, however, quite a number of plants that must have light to bring their seeds to life. When sowing the seed of these plants you should simply press them lightly into the growing medium and remember not to cover them.

Stages in the germination of a seed

Time necessary

Many seeds will germinate in a short time. In the right conditions many will germinate in as little as 5–10 days. Marigold, zinnia, cosmos, beans and peas are among this group. Other plants are quite slow, with parsley, begonia, pansy and cyclamen taking 3–4 weeks, some Australian native plants take 2–3 months and palms take up to 2 years.

Special requirements

Special treatment is needed to stimulate the seed of some plants into growth. Winter chilling or stratification is sometimes necessary, but there are also some arid region plants that need long periods of very dry heat to initiate germination. In their habitats these seeds lie dormant in the soil, baking through the dry hot summer, and are ready to germinate as soon as the first winter rains percolate down through the soil. Conditions then are cooler for the continued growth and development of the young seedlings. See the tip box opposite for the special temperature or light requirements of particular flowers, herbs and vegetables.

SPECIAL GERMINATION CONDITIONS

SEEDS THAT NEED LIGHT TO GERMINATE INCLUDE:
(flowers) ageratum, alyssum, aquilegia, begonia, coleus, impatiens, petunia, primula, snapdragon; (vegetables) lettuce

SEEDS THAT NEED WARMER TEMPERATURES INCLUDE:
(flowers) aster, celosia, coleus, petunia, verbena, zinnia; (vegetables) beans, capsicum, cucumber, eggplant, parsley, pumpkin, tomato

SEEDS THAT NEED COOLER TEMPERATURES INCLUDE:
(flowers) anemone, candytuft, dahlia, larkspur, nemesia, nigella, phlox; (herbs and vegetables) cress, coriander, lettuce, oregano, peas, spinach

Some plants need fire or smoke to break the dormancy of their seeds. Often fire is needed to open the seed capsules themselves (as for banksias, many wattles, South African proteas and ericas). This is the case with many plants from Australia and South Africa. It also applies to some plants of Mediterranean origin and from the south-west of the United States. These are all regions where fire is part of the natural cycle of the seasons. In the case of some plants, fire physically burns the woody seed-bearing organs, causing them to open and release the seed. This seed falls to the ground into the nutrient-rich ash left in the wake of the fire. The seed is therefore in an ideal spot for successful germination and growth when the first rainfall comes. Other plants have seed coats so hard that only burning by fire can make the coats permeable to moisture. Smoke without flame is also capable of stimulating germination of seeds in many of these plants.

GERMINATION TIPS

PROBLEMS WITH GROWING MEDIA, SOIL OR MIX

MAY BE TOO WET
Heavy, poorly drained soil or mix holds too much water, causing seeds to rot. You should use good-quality seed-raising mix or open up heavy soils by adding organic matter. Water only often enough to keep the seed moist but not wet.

MAY BE TOO DRY
Seeds cannot germinate without moisture. Once seeds swell and start to germinate they will die if they dry out. You should check moisture levels regularly. Cover sown seed with shadecloth, glass or even paper to conserve moisture.

SOIL-BORNE FUNGAL DISEASE
Sow seed only in fresh seed-raising mix in clean containers or in the garden in well-prepared, well-drained soil. Don't sow seed in areas where disease has been present. You should practise crop rotation to avoid continuing problems. Avoid overwatering and don't sow seed in poorly drained sites.

GROWING MEDIUM TOO LOOSE OR TOO COMPACTED
If you haven't firmed down the mix after seed sowing there will be too much air around the seed—this lack of contact with the mix means seed will dry out. If the mix is too compacted drainage will be poor and seeds will be deprived of oxygen.

PLANTING DEPTH
A good general rule of thumb for seed sowing is to plant at a depth of twice the diameter of the seed. Very fine seed of plants such as begonia and petunia should just be pressed into the surface of the mix. If you sow seed too deeply it may not have enough food reserves to provide the energy needed to reach the surface. Shallow-sown seed is more likely to rot if given constant watering. By the same token, if the sowing depth is too shallow the seed is at risk of drying out, unless you are vigilant about watering. The lower soil temperature at a greater depth may also affect germination.

It is possible for the home gardener to raise seed of plants requiring smoke for germination. The seed should be sown in pots or trays, and the container must be covered with a small 'tent'. Smoke generated by burning both dry and green leaves is then pumped into the covered tray. Once the smoking process has been completed, the smoke deposit is watered in. The active compounds contained in the smoke are now available as granular material that can be sprinkled on top of the seed-raising mix after sowing, then watered in. This treatment has produced a quite dramatic improvement in the germination rates of the seed of many species that had previously given disappointing results.

Other seeds need to be washed or soaked in order to germinate. In certain plants the hard seed coats may have to be filed, rubbed with fine sandpaper or nicked with a clean sharp knife to allow moisture to enter the seed.

TEMPERATURE

Few seeds germinate well in cold conditions. Each plant species has its optimum temperature range for germination. Certain plants such as poppy or nemesia like slightly cool conditions. By contrast, many summer-growing plant species such as beans, tomatoes, eggplant and cucumber, verbena, zinnia and petunia will germinate poorly (if in fact they germinate at all) in cool to cold conditions.

PESTS

Animals such as cats and dogs often dig up freshly tilled soil. It is therefore strongly recommended that you cover your seedbeds with wire netting to prevent this kind of damage. You can also place strong smelling mothballs or animal repellents around the bed to further discourage pets.

Snails and slugs can totally demolish young seedlings that are emerging from the soil. You can use physical barriers such as sharp shell grit scattered around the sown area, or you could sprinkle commercial snail baits on the seed bed. It is vital to ensure that neither children nor dogs are able to reach the baits.

FERTILISER

Fresh fertiliser in the soil can burn seeds and emerging roots. To avoid this problem, apply fertiliser in bands on either side of the planting row. You also have the choice of waiting until the seedlings have emerged and are growing strongly before you apply any fertiliser. Do not allow the fertiliser to touch the leaves or stems of the seedlings, as it could scorch them.

Alternatively, you can place the fertiliser in a furrow well below the seed-sowing area. Make the furrow about 8–10 cm deep, place the fertiliser along the trench, then backfill with soil. Firm the soil down with your hands and sow the seed.

SEED VIABILITY

The seeds of many plants lose their viability quite quickly once you have opened the sealed packet. Lettuce and parsnip are two plants that rapidly lose their freshness and ability to germinate. Generally, once you have opened the foil pack it is a good idea to try to use the seed within six months. Store seeds in a cool dry area to prolong the period of viability—both heat and moisture will cause rapid deterioration of seed.

Growing
on
seedlings

Many seeds can be planted directly where the plant will grow, but others need to be transferred as seedlings from the seed-raising container into the garden or permanent container. Container-grown seedlings must be pricked out and replanted in intermediate pots or trays until they are

growing strongly
enough to be
planted in their
permanent
position.

Pricking out

Container-grown seedlings must be thinned out to wider spacings once they are growing strongly. This process, which is known as pricking out, allows for optimum development of the seedling. If the seedlings are very crowded, prick them out as soon as you think they are large enough to handle. At this stage they will probably be about 15–20 mm high and have their first true leaves (that is, the leaves that emerge above the seed leaves). Plant them out in another container to grow on until they are ready for their intended growing positions. Seeds that have been planted at adequate spacings, usually large seeds, can be left to grow on where they are until they are 8–10 cm high. At that stage they will be ready to be planted out in their permanent positions either in the ground or in containers.

When you are pricking out and replanting these tiny seedlings, work out of the sun and out of the wind. Spread out a sheet of plastic or newspaper so that you have somewhere to place the small bundles of seedlings once they have been removed from the seed pots or trays.

Fill a seed tray or pot with a suitable potting mix and, using a pencil or stick, make holes in the mix ready to receive the little plants. Make the holes 3–6 cm apart. The wider spacing is needed for plants with large leaves such as lettuce, cabbage or foxglove.

Use a flat blade or a stick to separate and lift out a bunch of seedlings from their original container. Place them on the sheet of paper or plastic that you have previously spread out in readiness and gently separate them. Hold the seedling firmly but gently and lower its roots into the hole, then backfill the hole by pushing the potting mix around the roots with a stick or with your fingers.

PRICKING OUT

1

2

3

1 Gently hold onto the leaves (not the stem) and use a flat blade or stick to lift the seedling.

2 Make a planting hole in the new container with a pencil or stick.

3 Hold the seedling above the planting hole and lower its roots into the hole.

4 Gently press the damp growing mix around the seedling with your fingers.

5 After pricking out all the seedlings, gently water around the base of each plant to settle the mix.

4

5

Gently water the plants with a fine spray and set the container in a sheltered position. The container should receive some sun but preferably only early morning sun until the seedlings have recovered from their move.

Once the plants have recovered from transplanting shock, gradually expose them to more sunlight and give them some liquid fertiliser at half strength. When the plants are growing strongly and have reached a height of 8–10 cm they are ready to be planted in their permanent position.

Transplanting

When transplanting the seedlings into the ground or into their permanent containers, you should make sure that everything is ready before removing them from their trays or pots. Have the garden soil well prepared, marking out

TRANSPLANTING

1 Lift the seedling with a trowel or flat blade, leaving some soil around the roots.

2 Lower the plant into the hole and firm the soil around it.

3 Provide some shade with leaves or with grass until the plant is established in its new position.

planting holes with a narrow-bladed trowel or your fingers.

Lift the seedlings with a trowel or flat blade, disturbing the roots as little as possible and leaving soil attached to the plant roots. Lower the plant into the hole and firm the soil around the roots, leaving a small depression around the plant to ensure that water is directed to the root zone. Give the plant a thorough watering. If you have some old compost or manure you can sprinkle this around the plants as a mulch to help conserve moisture—just make sure that you leave a little space around the plant stem. It may also be a good idea for you to sprinkle some snail bait around the newly planted seedlings, especially if the weather is damp or dewy.

In hot weather do your transplanting in the evening as this allows plants some time to recuperate. Plants may well wilt the following day when the full heat of the sun is upon them, but if the soil is moist they should recover once the sun moves off them. If it is extremely hot you could consider providing plants with some form of shading through the middle of the day.

Watering and fertilising

Watering at this stage is also very important, but you should check the soil by scratching away the surface to feel or see whether it is still damp. As you want to encourage plants to put down deep roots it is better to soak the area every few days rather than sprinkle it daily. Of course, the frequency of watering will depend on the season and the weather.

After a few days, when the seedlings have recovered from the move, you should give them a dose of half strength liquid plant food. It is also important to keep the area free of weeds so that the young plants are not competing for water or nutrients.

Soils and potting mixes

Good preparation of your soil or careful selection of a light, loose, free-draining mix will make it easier for the seed to germinate and result in a better success rate for seed raising. You can make your own seed-raising mixes, or purchase a commercially available mix; bear in mind that it is only meant as a starting medium, and usually won't be suitable for long-term growth.

Soil types

Different types of soil have different properties. Different regions have different soils depending on the type of rock from which they were formed. It is worth knowing what type of soil you have in your garden.

• Clay soil compacts when dry and becomes waterlogged with too much moisture but it does have the ability to hold nutrients well. Drainage and aeration are both poor and it is very difficult for roots of young plants to move through this type of soil.

• Sandy soil never compacts and it provides excellent aeration and drainage. However, it has no ability to hold nutrients or water.

• Loam is a combination of clay and sandy soil with excellent properties for plant growth. However, few gardeners are blessed with this ideal soil type.

The potting mixes that you purchase from a garden centre contain no soil. They comprise a uniform mix of components that are necessary for plant growth.

Improving soil

All soils can be improved by the addition of large quantities of organic matter, whether it is well-decayed compost or manure. Organic matter helps to break up heavy clay and aids in moisture retention in sandy soil. In winter, organic matter should be dug into the ground 4–6 weeks before planting and in summer about 3 weeks before planting. In addition, organic materials can be used as mulches around plants once they are established.

Heavy clay soil can also be improved by the addition of gypsum at a rate of about 300 g per square metre. Gypsum is a naturally occurring compound of calcium sulphate that has no harmful effect whatsoever on the soil or the

Plants requiring free-draining soil will thrive when grown as part of a rock garden

environment—it helps to break up the clay so that aeration and drainage are both improved. Not all clay soils benefit from the addition of gypsum, but many of them do.

Drainage

The vast majority of plants that you may want to grow will need to be planted in soil that drains well. Although there are plants that thrive in permanently moist or boggy soil, most annual flowers and certainly all vegetable crops need free-draining soil.

Check the drainage before you start to prepare the soil. This is a simple matter. Dig a hole 20–30 cm deep and fill it with water. If there is still water in the hole five or six hours later then drainage is poor. If there is still water in the hole twelve hours or more longer you will have problems establishing a garden in that location. For satisfactory results you will have to raise the bed, retaining the soil with bricks or timber.

Preparing the ground

To prepare for planting, the soil should be dug over to a depth of 20–25 cm (about spade depth) so that any lumps or clods can be broken up. The subsoil should not be disturbed during this digging. Whether you are preparing to sow seed directly into the bed or preparing to plant seedlings, the finished result should be roughly the same. Having broken up any lumps in the soil, add organic matter and then water the whole area.

After you have incorporated organic matter into the soil you should leave the bed for about two weeks during summer and for 4–6 weeks in winter to allow the added material to begin breaking down. If you are preparing the ground for a vegetable garden you will need to incorporate a large quantity of organic material into the ground. In high rainfall areas or where soils are known to be very acid, it is often a good idea to add agricultural lime or dolomite to the soil before planting vegetables. This need only be done every year or two. The quantity required depends on the soil type. Some crops, notably those in the cabbage family, need a neutral or slightly alkaline soil for best results. After the bed has been left for the required period of time, go back and lightly dig over the ground. The soil should have a crumbly surface layer and should not compact or form a crust. Rake over the surface to even out any bumps, then with the back of the rake smooth it over so that you have a nice level piece of ground ready to receive seed or seedlings.

Cultivation to produce a fine surface layer of soil is especially important when you are sowing the seed directly into the ground.

Seed-raising mixes

For seed raising in trays or pots you can make your own mix or purchase a ready-made commercial seed-raising mix. These mixes are ideal for germinating seed and raising seedlings of flowers and vegetables, but are not generally suitable for long-term growth. There is not enough body in the mix in the way of organic matter to hold water and nutrients to maintain plants over a long growing season.

The simplest seed-raising mix is made up of two parts coarse washed river sand or propagating sand with one part of peat moss or coconut fibre peat. You will find that these items are readily available from nurseries and garden centres. Beach sand is unsuitable for use in seed-raising mixes, as is builders' sand which sets like concrete once it has been wet and dries again. Coconut or coir fibre peat is often sold as cocopeat. Well-aged, crumbly garden compost can be used as a substitute for the peat.

Vermiculite is also used in seed-raising mixes as it is able to absorb large quantities of water and can hold nutrients in reserve for the developing seedlings. Vermiculite is expanded mica, and tiny plant roots are able to penetrate its particles. It never cakes and, although quite expensive, can be a useful addition to mixes. Because it is light coloured and shiny it is also useful to sprinkle over a row of seed sown into the ground as it stops the surface caking and readily marks the rows. Sand can also be used for marking rows as well as for preventing caking.

Perlite is another good addition to seed-raising mixes although it too is quite expensive. Perlite is of volcanic origin and is mined from lava flows. It is extremely light but can hold 3–4 times its own weight of water. It has no nutrients but aids in the aeration of mixes.

Perlite or vermiculite would generally be used in seed-raising mixes at the ratio of 1 part added to 2 parts of sand.

Fertiliser should not be added to seed-raising mixes as a rule as the seeds themselves cannot use the fertiliser and young emerging roots may be burnt if they come into contact with it.

Garden soil, however good it is in the garden, is generally unsuitable for seed raising. Both drainage and aeration can be poor, leading to very low seed germination rates. Seed-raising media must always drain well and be well aerated. Even the best soil tends to compact to a certain degree when placed in containers. It is also impossible to guarantee that garden soil does not contain pathogens. Soil should only be used if it is pasteurised, which means that it has been kept at a temperature of 60°C for 30 minutes to kill off any pathogens. Soil can be baked in the oven or in a microwave, but you should note that this is a messy business and the soil will still be unsuitable for using on its own for seed raising.

Buying mixes

It is generally much cheaper and a great deal easier to buy ready-made potting mixes than to make up your own. As well as the cost of the raw materials there is the question of space to store them and in which to actually put the mix together.

Ready-made mixes available from garden centres and nurseries should contain all the physical and chemical properties necessary for good plant growth. If you buy mixes made to a standard specification (this is stated on the bag) you should not have any problems.

Mixes may be labelled standard or premium. The main difference is that premium mixes contain added nutrients to sustain plant growth for several weeks or months. With standard mixes you are getting a mix with good physical properties to which you can add fertiliser as you want. Generally mixes from the same manufacturer have the same physical properties whether they are standard or premium.

Most mixes can be used straight from the bag or they can be modified to suit your needs. The majority of bagged potting mixes contain composted pine bark as the major component. Some use a proportion of composted sawdust, sand or peat. If you want a more moisture-retentive mix you can add coconut fibre peat, peat moss, or aged compost and manure. Adding about one-third by volume of any of these components should ensure better moisture retention without impeding drainage. To make the mix more open for succulent plants, coarse sand or gravel can be incorporated. Mixes for specific plant types, such as orchids, cactus and succulents, are available.

You can also obtain formulations containing a higher proportion of organic matter which makes them most suitable for use in exposed conditions where pots are liable to dry out rapidly. Some mixes contain water-retentive gels or granules. This means that the plants will need watering less frequently. These mixes are especially useful for planting up hanging baskets, which can dry out very quickly.

A good potting mix should be well aerated and drain well but it should also be easy to re-wet after drying. Although the mix will gradually break down over time it should not show undue shrinkage over the first six months or so. A potting mix formulated to standard specifications should be free of pathogens and have a pH (degree of acidity or alkalinity) suitable for the growth of a wide range of plants. pH is measured in units from 1 to 14, with 7 being neutral. A level of 1 is very acid, while a level of 14 is extremely alkaline.

Preparing the container

Modern potting mixes are such that there is no need to use crocks over the drain holes of pots. If your container has particularly large drain holes these can be covered with a piece of flyscreen wire or shade cloth before adding the mix.

If you are planting a number of seedlings into a container it is probably best to fill the container to within 2 or 3 cm of the top and then use a stick or your fingers to make holes into which the seedlings can be inserted. On the other hand, if you are planting larger plants into individual pots it may be best to fill the pot to two-thirds of its height and then, holding the plant in one hand, you can use your other hand or a scoop to add extra potting mix. The finished planting should bring the mix to within 2 or 3 cm of the pot rim to allow for efficient watering. If the pot is overfilled, water may run off the surface rather than soak into the mix.

GENERAL CULTIVATION

WATERING

Watering seems to be the aspect of cultivation that causes the gardener the most problems. The best advice is to use your commonsense. Consider the time of year, temperature, humidity, time of day, weather, soil conditions and the stage of development of the plant.

Seeds cannot germinate without moisture. Keep the seed-raising mix evenly moist but not wet until seedlings emerge. Once seedlings emerge, water them regularly and gently with a fine spray. You should be aware that overwatering will cause the collapse and death of seedlings. Once seedlings have been planted out they will need regular watering until they are well established.

The age and type of plant will also affect the amount of water required. Baby seedlings with very few shallow roots will need more frequent watering than established plants that have their roots deeper into the ground. Plants with large leaves generally need more water than those with fine feathery leaves. Annual flowers and vegetables may need watering twice a week, weekly or every two or three days depending on weather and soil conditions. You should note that sandy soils dry out much more rapidly than clay soils.

It is generally more effective to water early in the morning or in the evening, as there will be less moisture lost through evaporation at these times. In winter most watering should be done in the morning so that the foliage does not remain wet overnight. This also applies to plants that are prone to fungal disease—avoid overhead watering for these plants. In summer it is a good idea to water in the evening so the water has a chance to soak into the ground. It is unwise to water in the middle of the day in summer or when it is very windy, as a lot of water will be lost to the atmosphere straight away.

FERTILISING

Keep your seedlings growing rapidly by carrying out regular fertilising. Vegetables especially must be grown quickly for maximum flavour and tenderness. There are several methods of maintaining a steady supply of nutrients to your seedlings.

Granular fertiliser can be used prior to seed sowing by banding it along the sides of rows or by placing it in a furrow or trench well below the seed sowing depth. Soluble powders or liquid concentrates, which you need to dilute and apply in solution, can be used to boost plant growth once seedlings are growing strongly. Slow release fertilisers can be mixed with the soil or potting mix prior to sowing or applied once seedlings have started to grow.

Never apply fertiliser to dry soil as there is a good chance this will burn the plant roots.

While it is preferable to feed plants through their roots, some growers like to use foliar feeding (feeding plants through their leaves). When using fertiliser in solution to spray directly onto leaves, there should be plenty of moisture around the plant roots.

PESTS AND DISEASES

PESTS

CURLED OR DISTORTED LEAVES

Look for aphids, which are small sticky insects that cluster under leaves. Aphids may be green, pink, black, grey or yellowish in colour.
PLANTS AFFECTED: Many including aster, broad bean, broccoli, cabbage, carrot, cauliflower, cornflower, foxglove, stock, viola.
CONTROL: Wash aphids off the plant with a hose; you can also spray with insecticidal soap, pyrethrum or imidacloprid (Confidor®).

BRONZED, MOTTLED LEAVES

Generally caused by mites, especially two-spotted mites, that suck sap from foliage. Damage occurs mostly in hot dry conditions.
PLANTS AFFECTED: Almost any plant may be attacked especially if plants are under stress.
CONTROL: Overhead watering helps, as does hosing up under the leaves. Spray the affected plant with dicofol (Kelthane®) or fluvilinate (Mavrik®).

SILVERY TRAILS IN LEAF TISSUE

Leafminers, tiny caterpillars that 'mine' between leaf surfaces, cause disfiguration of leaves.
PLANTS AFFECTED: Cineraria, marguerite daisy, silver beet and spinach.
CONTROL: Spray with omethoate (Folimat®) or dimethoate (Rogor®). You should check the withholding period for vegetables.

HOLES IN LEAVES OR LEAF EDGES CHEWED

• May be caused by snails or slugs. Silvery trails are often seen.
PLANTS AFFECTED: All plants can be grazed by snails and slugs.
CONTROL: Search for and destroy snails or make physical barriers of dry sawdust or shell grit around young seedlings. Use baits containing metaldehyde or methiocarb but keep baits away from children or dogs.
• Caterpillars chew leaves of plants. They are often well camouflaged.
PLANTS AFFECTED: All plants are susceptible to caterpillar damage. Some caterpillars are host specific; for example, the cabbage white butterfly larva damages only flowers and vegetables in the crucifer group (which includes plants such as broccoli, cabbage, cress and radish).
CONTROL: Dust plants on several consecutive nights with rotenone (derris dust) or pyrethrum or spray with the bio-insecticide *Bacillus thuringiensis* (Dipel®). If damage persists spray plants with carbaryl.

WHITE FLUFFY PATCHES ON LEAVES, STEMS OR ROOTS

Mealybugs are not a common problem on plants that are grown outdoors although potted plants may be more susceptible. They thrive in warm moist conditions. Mealybugs resemble small sticky blobs of cotton wool.
PLANTS AFFECTED: Any plant may be attacked but polyanthus seem particularly susceptible.
CONTROL: Spray plants with imidacloprid (Confidor®).

SEEDLINGS CUT OFF AT GROUND LEVEL

Cutworms are often responsible, but snails can also cause this problem. Cutworms hide in the soil by day, emerging to feed at night.
PLANTS AFFECTED: All plants can be attacked by cutworms.
CONTROL: Dust seedlings with rotenone (derris dust) or carbaryl on several consecutive nights.

DISEASES

COLLAPSE AND DEATH OF SEEDS AND SEEDLINGS

Damping off is a disease caused by a soil-borne fungus. It is encouraged by overwet soils and very humid conditions. Damping off occurs more often when seeds have been sown too thickly. It can kill seeds before they germinate or young seedlings after they have emerged through the soil. The fungus can remain active in the soil even after the affected seedlings have been removed. The use of new, fresh seed-raising mix will help prevent the occurrence of damping off.
PLANTS AFFECTED: All plants are susceptible to damping off.
CONTROL: Difficult to eradicate, but drenching soil with furalaxyl (Fongarid®) helps give protection.

GREY/WHITE POWDER ON LEAF SURFACES

Mostly caused by powdery mildew, a common fungal disease that is a perennial problem in humid districts.
PLANTS AFFECTED: Many including begonia, calendula, dahlia, sweet pea, zinnia, cucumber, marrow, melon, pea, pumpkin, squash and zucchini.
CONTROL: Plant resistant varieties where possible. Dust or spray plants with sulphur if temperature is below 28°C, or spray with triadimefon (Baycor®) or triforine.

YELLOWISH MOTTLE ON UPPER LEAF; RUSTY, BROWN SPOTS ON UNDERSIDE

These are symptoms of rust, a fungal disease. There are many strains of rust but each attacks only a specific few plant types. Spores are spread by wind and water splash.
PLANTS AFFECTED: A large range including calendula, carnation, geranium, hollyhock, snapdragon and bean.
CONTROL: Remove the worst affected leaves and avoid overhead watering. Spray or dust plants with copper oxychloride or mancozeb.

BLACK OR BROWN SPOTS ON LEAVES

Usually symptoms of one of the many leaf-spotting fungal diseases. Some strains attack a wide range of plants, others are host specific. Spores are spread by wind and water splash.
PLANTS AFFECTED: Many including dahlia, gerbera, beetroot, celery, pea, silver beet and spinach.
CONTROL: Avoid watering foliage where possible and don't water late in the day. Copper-based sprays and mancozeb control fungal leaf spots.

FLOWERS

Flowers provide colour and interesting accents in the garden, and they can also be cut and brought indoors to brighten our homes. You may choose to plant flower mixes to create a kaleidoscope of colour, or decide on a restrained scheme of perhaps only two or three colours. Some gardeners opt for flowers of a single shade, especially if they want a very stylish or formal effect. Seeds of many flowers are available in both mixed and single colours. Seed packets also often give planting suggestions to help you create a lovely floral display.

There is a much wider range of flowers available as seed than will ever be found as seedlings for sale in nurseries. Many unusual plants and unusual varieties of commonly grown flowering plants are available in seed form. To add perfume to the garden, try some of the lovely scented annuals that can be grown from seed. There is a wonderful range of old-fashioned sweet peas that are richly fragrant. Stock, carnation, pink, dianthus, sweet William and lavender are all scented, while other annual plants such as alyssum, pansy and verbena have lighter scents.

No other plants give your garden the splashes of colour and seasonal interest that annuals do. You can plant annuals in beds on their own, as borders to shrub plantings, as fillers and as accent plants in pots and hanging baskets.

Annuals are plants that mature, flower and seed in one season or year. They are generally planted twice a year, in autumn and spring. Autumn-sown annuals provide flowers through late winter and spring: plants such as alyssum, pansy and viola will carry the garden right through spring with regular dead-heading (that is, removing spent flowers). Spring-sown annuals give garden colour in summer and autumn: long-flowering annuals that continue through summer into autumn include cosmea, salvia, petunia, marigold and zinnia. Planting continues through summer to provide a continuous display of colour in the garden when most people are spending time outdoors, so taking the garden through into autumn.

While perennials remain alive for a number of years, biennials complete their life cycle in two years, growing the first year and flowering and producing seed in the second year. Many of these flowering perennials are planted in autumn to allow establishment before winter slows growth; more plants are suited to autumn planting than to spring planting. Many

lovely flowering plants are perennials, which have the advantage that they do not need to be replaced frequently. Perennials vary greatly in their size, foliage type, flower shape and colour. Mixed perennials are often planted in borders or garden beds on their own but can also be used among annuals, shrubs or bulbs. Most are suitable for growing in containers. Many perennials are herbaceous, growing rapidly through spring and early summer to flower later in summer or autumn. Herbaceous plants die back to the roots or fleshy crown and remain dormant during winter or, in some cases, during what would be their dry season in nature. In spring new growth appears from the previously dormant rootstock. Many perennials have their origins in cool climates, where they will die back completely in autumn. The same plants grown in warm climates may not become completely dormant over winter.

TRANSPLANTING SEEDLINGS

Using a trowel or your hand, dig a hole 7–10 cm deep for each seedling. Gently ease out seedlings from the seed box or punnet, taking as much soil as possible with each one. Place the seedling in the hole, press soil around it and make a saucer-shaped depression at the same time to direct water to the roots. Spread compost or dry grass clippings around each seedling, then water in using a watering can or a slow-running hose.

In summer it is best to transplant in late afternoon or evening. If transplanting during the day, shade each seedling with a piece of brush or a handful of long, dry grass or straw.

A SAMPLE FLOWER BED

SPRING THROUGH SUMMER

Salvia

Sweet William

Marigold

Floss flower

Snapdragon

Pansy

Lobelia

Verbena

Viola

AUTUMN THROUGH WINTER

Calendula

Poppy

Snapdragon

Primula

Dianthus

Pansy

Viola

It is important, especially in the case of annuals, to plant at the correct time of year. Some annuals will not flower if the day length or temperature is unsuitable. Follow the seed packet directions and our planting guide and you should have success. When annuals are planted out of season, seed may fail to germinate, or if it does, growth may be short lived. Plants that continue growing may not flower.

To get the maximum flowering from your display, don't allow plants to flower when they are very small. As buds appear, pinch them out with your fingertips. If you allow annuals to flower when they are tiny they will never develop into good-sized plants and will be only short lived. Pinching out the growing tips of many plants is also a good idea, as this helps to create a bushier plant. Regular dead-heading will help to prolong your floral display. You need to go over your plants about once a week and cut off the spent flowers; if you don't remove them, the plant will divert its resources into setting seed and will stop producing a fresh crop of flowers. If you are cutting flowers for the vase, do so early in the morning or late in the afternoon. Cool them down quickly by placing them in a bucket of cool water in a cool place, and leave them for an hour or so before arranging them.

ACHILLEA 'CLOTH OF GOLD'
This easy-care perennial with its flat heads of bright golden yellow flowers will bring colour to the garden over a long period. The vivid yellow of the flowers teams well with other hot colours such as red and orange but could be planted in contrast to blue and white flowers too. The feathery foliage is also decorative. Best planted in large drifts, it is a tall grower to around 1 m high. Plants spread by runners so should be planted 25–30 cm apart. However, for

Achillea 'Cloth of Gold'

quick effect they can be planted closer as thinning is quite easy. The long-lasting flowers are ideal cut for the vase but will last longer in the garden. This plant will grow in any kind of well-drained soil in most climates except the tropics. It is best in full sun although it will tolerate shade for part of the day.

SEASON: Seeds are planted in late autumn to early winter. Flowers should appear in the following summer.

AGERATUM
Also known as floss flower, ageratum bears masses of fluffy flowers over a long period. In warm climates it may be in flower from early spring through to autumn, especially if plants are cut back after the first flowering is over. Flowers come in a range of soft shades of blue, mauve, pink and white and their cool colours can be a welcome contrast to other, brighter flowers. This easy-to-grow annual can be used for edging garden beds, in massed displays and as a container plant. Flowers can be cut for the vase and last quite well if the stems are scalded after picking and before soaking in cool water. Tolerant of sun or light shade, it can be grown in almost any kind of well-drained soil. It can be sown virtually all year round except in

Top: Ageratum 'Blue Mink'
Above: 'Swing'

districts that have late frosts. Plants are generally spaced 10–15 cm apart.
SEASON: Can be sown year round in warm climates, middle to late spring in cool zones. From seed to flowering takes about 12 weeks.

Ageratum 'Blue Mink'

This compact form grows from 20 to 30 cm high. The rounded fluffy flowers are soft powder blue, making it ideal for inclusion in pastel colour schemes.

Ageratum 'Swing'

This seed mix will give you a pastel border all from one packet. Flowers range through pink, lilac, lavender and blue. They are borne on very dwarf plants 15–20 cm high. This mix is ideal for containers on balconies as the variety can help create the feeling of a larger garden.

ALSTROEMERIA LIGTU HYBRIDS

Once you grow this lovely herbaceous perennial you will have your own supply of cut flowers over many weeks each year from late spring through summer. Sometimes known as the Peruvian lily, this hybrid selection brings you the best colour selection with flowers in pink, salmon, red, orange and yellow. The trumpet-shaped flowers on stems 50–70 cm high are marked in the throat with contrasting streaks and spots of colour. Plants should be grown in a sheltered position in sun or very light shade only. Soil should be well prepared before planting out as plants can remain in their positions for several years without division. The ideal soil is well drained and rich in organic matter. Plants benefit from mulching in high summer. When seedlings are large enough for their permanent positions they should be spaced about 30 cm apart. This plant is not suitable for the tropics or for outdoor cultivation in very cold areas. Seeds are sown from late summer to early spring. Mid-winter is best avoided.
SEASON: Sow late summer to early spring. The flowers first appear 18–20 weeks after sowing.

Alstroemeria Ligtu hybrids

ALYSSUM

One of the most widely grown of annuals, alyssum or sweet Alice is familiar to most gardeners in white or dark violet used as an edging plant. This is, however, far from the whole colour range or variety of applications for today's lovely versatile plants. There is now a far greater colour range and plants may be used in all kinds of ways. It is still a lovely edging plant and is used in carpet bedding and general displays of annuals. You can grow these plants in pots and hanging baskets, in rockeries, in cracks in paving, just about anywhere you want a little colour and variety. Flowers have a light honey scent and last for many weeks.

Plants are best grown in full sun and will do well in almost any kind of well-drained soil. Heights vary from 7 to 15 cm high depending on variety. Plants are generally spaced 7–10 cm apart but this can be varied according to the effect being sought. Where possible, seed should be sown directly where it is to grow. Shear plants after the initial flowering to keep them compact and promote further flower. Alyssum does well in both cool and warm zones but it is generally unsuitable for growing in the tropics.

SEASON: Seed can be sown year round in most climates. Growth is rapid and plants should flower within 8 weeks of sowing.

Alyssum 'Aphrodite'

This is a mini-garden in one packet of seed. While it makes a good edging or border plant it is ideal for troughs and pots, combining many colours on compact plants growing only about 8 cm high. The colour range includes white, yellow, apricot, salmon, red, pink and purple, forming a tapestry in bloom. Plants spaced not much more than 7 cm apart will create an unbroken carpet of bloom.

Alyssum 'Carpet of Snow'

'Carpet of Snow', as its name suggests, is the whitest of white flowers. Wherever this is planted it gives a lift to the garden. Its bright white makes a lovely contrast for brightly coloured flowers and it is ideal for providing contrast with mainly green plants. The rounded heads of tiny flowers are a good foil for heavier looking annuals such as stock or ranunculus, or even violas and pansies. Interesting patterns can be made with this alyssum and royal blue lobelia 'Crystal Palace', which has compact growth of about the same height.

Alyssum 'Creamery'

This lovely soft cream alyssum will be welcomed by gardeners who feel that stark white is too harsh for their colour schemes. It might also be used in a colour scheme grading from pure white through to yellow and pale orange. Like most varieties of alyssum this is a compact grower to about 8 cm with a long flowering period. It would make a fine accompaniment to any of the Californian poppies from the bright orange to the more subtle tones of the 'Prima Ballerina' mix or the mixed singles. Its versatility makes it a must for inclusion in spring and summer gardens.

Alyssum 'Golf Rose'

Slightly taller than some varieties of alyssum, this grows to about 12 cm high with distinctly pink flowers that are paler in the centre. Equally suitable for edging, bedding or container growing, it teams well with a wide range of spring or summer flowering annuals and perennials. Try this with mixed asters in summer or with Virginian stock in spring.

Alyssum 'Royal Carpet'

A favourite over many years, 'Royal Carpet' is possibly second only to 'Carpet

Top left to right: Alyssum 'Aphrodite', 'Carpet of Snow', 'Creamery'. Centre left to right: 'Golf Rose'; 'Royal Carpet'. Above left to right: 'Saxatile Gold Dust'; 'Trailing Rosy Red'

of Snow' in popularity. The two are often planted together. The deep violet flowers of 'Royal Carpet' tend to be white in the centre so tying the two in together. Both grow to around 8 cm in height with each plant spreading 20–25 cm. Often used in large scale plantings in parks and public gardens, this is a hardy plant able to cope with harsh conditions once established.

Alyssum 'Saxatile Gold Dust'

This small rounded perennial grows 20–30 cm high. It sometimes forms a mound 40–50 cm across but often tends to spread more loosely to a similar spread. Its bright gold flowers and grey-green foliage make it a lovely foil for dark-foliaged shrubs or as an edging plant for a large tub. It likes a sunny spot and must have fast draining soil. It will grow among rocks or on a sloping bank which mimics its habitat in central and southern Europe. Although classed as a frost hardy perennial it is often grown as an annual. It should be cut back after its spring flowering to keep the plant compact. Seed can be sown all year round but it is most often sown during late summer or autumn for flowers in the following spring.

Alyssum 'Trailing Rosy Red'

For gardeners familiar with white or purple alyssum, this is a real surprise. This new variety of annual alyssum is a pretty deep rose to red, lasting over very many weeks. Its low growth (8–10 cm) and trailing habit make it ideal for growing in hanging baskets or to edge larger pots. It is also lovely planted in rockeries and at the edge of low retaining walls where its softening effect will be appreciated. In good conditions each plant may spread to 50 cm so that in the open garden plants may be more widely spaced than most alyssum. By sowing at 15–20 cm intervals or more you should get good cover.

AQUILEGIA

Old fashioned favourites that are also known as columbines or granny's bonnets, aquilegias are herbaceous perennials often grown as annuals. A must for cottage gardens, they are also ideal for woodland gardens, especially for planting under deciduous trees. Plants flower in middle to late spring in warm districts and in summer in cool areas. Plants form a rosette of pretty grey-green foliage from which the flower stems rise. Plants may last only 2–3 years but are easy to raise from seed. Flowers cut well for the vase but the display will be much longer lasting in the garden. Best grown

Top: Aquilegia 'McKana Giant Hybrids'
Above: 'Nora Barlow—The Mixture'

in semi-shade they will take full sun in cool regions. They prefer a humus-rich soil that drains well. Keep plants well watered in dry weather and mulch to keep roots cool. Space plants at 30–40 cm intervals but plant in groups of at least three plants to achieve a pretty effect.
SEASON: Sow in autumn or early spring. From seed to flowering may take from 20 to 25 weeks.

Aquilegia 'McKana Giant Hybrids'

The long-spurred flowers of these modern hybrids come in a wonderful colour range that includes white, pink, crimson, yellow and blue, as well as combinations of two contrasting tones or two shades of one colour. Plants grow 40–70 cm high.

Aquilegia 'Nora Barlow–The Mixture'

This seed mix from the Granny's Garden range is a treat for lovers of old-fashioned flowers and for those wanting to create a traditional cottage garden. It is a collection of mainly double, spurless flower forms that are the true granny's bonnets of yesteryear. 'Nora Barlow' is a quaint and pretty double flower that is a curious mix of red, pink and green. Other flowers in this mix may be blue, purple, pink, cream or white. Plants grow 60–90 cm tall.

ARABIS 'PINK SNOW'

Arabis or rock cress is a delightful little perennial plant to fill pockets in rockeries or drystone walls or to use simply as a groundcover. 'Pink Snow' will carpet the ground and be almost smothered in rosy pink flowers like single stocks through spring and continuing into summer in cooler regions. Flowers are lightly scented. Arabis teams well with carnations and pinks, which enjoy the same growing conditions. Growing only 15–20 cm high, each plant should spread

Arabis 'Pink Snow'

30 or 40 cm. Space seeds about 20 cm apart. Best in full sun, it must have perfectly drained soil. Lime should be added to very acid soils before planting. After flowering, cut back to ensure bushy, compact growth. As long as drainage is good this plant is easy to grow in cool or warm regions but not the tropics.
SEASON: Sow seed in autumn or early winter for flowering the following spring and summer. In cold areas seed may also be sown in spring.

ASTER

With regular cutting for the vase and dead-heading, annual China asters will flower right through summer into autumn. They make a brilliant garden display with their large flowers in shades of pink, purple, crimson and white. Plant in full sun in well-drained soil that has been enriched with organic matter. Provide wind protection for tall varieties and mulch around the root zones. Make sure they are given ample water in dry weather. Tall growers can be spaced 40 cm apart, dwarf forms about 20 cm apart.
SEASON: Sow in early spring in warm areas, later spring in cool zones. From seed to flower takes about 16 weeks.

Aster 'Californian Giant'

This strain of the China aster will grow 60 cm or more high, bearing large ruffled flowers in pink, purple, crimson and white through summer into autumn. This is an excellent cut flower and a showy border plant.

Aster 'Colour Carpet Mixed'

This dwarf variety grows only 20 cm high making a neat mound of colour when in bloom. Flower colours are the same as those of the taller varieties, and although flowers are on short stems they can be cut for posies or small vases. Being a small grower it can be grown in more exposed sites than the taller forms. Ideal for edging garden beds, it makes a delightful container plant too.

AUBRIETIA 'RICH ROSE'

This is an attractive mat-forming or carpeting perennial that grows only about 10 cm high but which in suitable conditions may spread 40–50 cm. It is best grown in full sun. It thrives in pockets of rockeries or tucked into spaces in retaining walls where drainage is rapid. While many forms of aubrietia have mauve or purple flowers, this is a very choice selection with masses of bright magenta to deep rose-pink flowers appearing in spring. Flowers last throughout spring and there is often spot flowering through summer into autumn. Shear over plants after flowering to promote plenty of new growth. Seed is sown in autumn to early winter, ideally where it is to grow although it can be sown in pots or trays. Spring sowings can also be made in cool areas. Unsuitable for the tropics or other warm regions of high humidity, it does best in cooler regions.
SEASON: Seed sown in autumn should bloom the following spring.

Top: Aster 'Californian Giant'
Above: 'Colour Carpet Mixed'

Aubrietia 'Rich Rose'

BALSAM 'CAMELLIA FLOWERED MIXED'

The flowers of this pretty annual are more similar to baby roses than camellias. Cultivated as glasshouse plants in cool climates, they are lovely plants for gardens and containers in warm regions. The ruffled flowers are borne singly or in clusters at the leaf junctions (nodes) over a long period. Flowers are pink, red, purple, white or sometimes bi-coloured. This is a just the plant to bring some colour to shaded sections of the garden through summer and autumn. Plants can be grown in sun with wind protection but are best shaded from hot afternoon sun. Growing to about 45 cm high they should be planted 20 cm apart in rich, well-drained soil. Container grown plants can be planted more closely. Regular dead-heading will prolong blooming.

SEASON: Sow seed in spring through to autumn in very warm districts for flowering 10–12 weeks later. In cool zones sow in late spring.

Balsam 'Camellia Flowered Mixed'

BEGONIA 'SUMMER RAINBOW'

Grown in sun or shade this bedding begonia will give months of colour in the garden or in containers. The slightly succulent leaves are almost obscured with masses of small, waxy flowers in shades of red, pink or white flowers. It makes a neat edging plant and is often used in carpet bedding but is equally at home in troughs and pots. Plants grow about 20 cm high and can be quite bushy so they should be spaced 20–25 cm apart. It is versatile enough to be grown in sun or shade but plants may be leggy and open if the shade is too heavy. The very fine seed should be sown and barely pressed into the seed-raising mix as it needs light to germinate. Once seedlings are large enough to handle they should be pricked out and grown on until they are large enough to weather the outdoors. Seed can be sown from spring to early summer in most regions but can be sown in autumn where winters are mild. This is an easy-care plant that gives great value for any effort put into raising it.

SEASON: Sow seed in spring to early summer in most regions. Seed may take 3–4 weeks to germinate. Expect plants to flower 12–14 weeks after sowing.

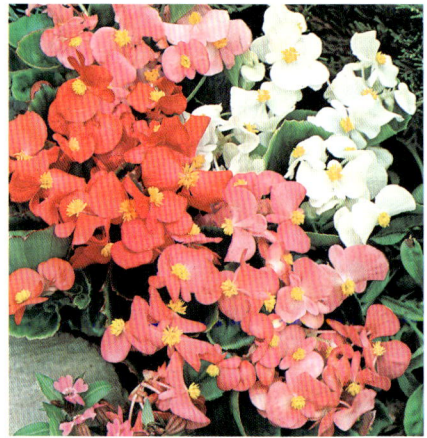

Begonia 'Summer Rainbow'

BELLS OF IRELAND

This mix is from Mr. Fothergill's Flower Arrangers range. Also known as molucca balm or shell flower, these plants are very popular with flower arrangers as they are used both fresh and dried to create unusual floral decorations. The shell-like green 'flowers' are actually the calyces of the inconspicuous true flowers. This tall-growing plant can reach 60–90 cm in height and so needs to be grown with protection from strong wind. Space plants 25–30 cm apart in well-drained soil in an open, sunny position. Although tolerant of any soil that drains well, growth will be improved if the soil is enriched with organic matter. This is a quick-growing annual that will look attractive in the garden over most of summer. Spikes are cut for the vase when the flowers on top of the spike are only just open. These spikes dry to a light buff-brown colour but they are still very decorative. Florists remove all the leaves from the spikes to display the unusual flowers to best effect.

SEASON: Seed is sown in spring for flowering during the summer months. Flowers should appear about 12 weeks after sowing.

Bells of Ireland

BIDENS 'GOLDEN GODDESS'

This quick-growing annual is ideal for container growing, either in pots or hanging baskets. The foliage is fine and feathery while the small yellow flowers are borne in clusters up to 5 cm across. Flowers appear from midsummer through to autumn. If plants are cut back after the first flowering flush, a second crop should appear within a few weeks. Bidens has a slightly trailing habit, growing from 40 to 60 cm in height. It would look pretty mixed with trailing lobelia or planted among marigolds to add a light contrast with their heavier looking flowers. 'Golden Goddess' is best sown in full sun where it is to grow as it is generally trouble-free and germinates easily. Space plants about 25 cm apart. Bidens should grow well in any kind of well-drained soil.

SEASON: Seed can be sown year round but is probably best sown in spring. the plants should reach flowering size 8 weeks after sowing.

Bidens 'Golden Goddess'

CABBAGE 'ORNAMENTAL TOKYO MIXED F1'

The colourful heads of this ornamental cabbage are always a talking point whether grown in the garden or individually in pots. Forming a rounded loose rosette of leaves, this particular strain has blue-green outer leaves with pink, red or white centres. Colour intensifies as the plants mature. As an F1 hybrid selection, plants are uniform and vigorous in growth. These make a novel edging plant or they could be planted on their own to create a carpet of interesting and colourful patterns. They need plenty of sun to develop good colour. While the leaves are edible they have a very bitter taste. Like all members of the cabbage family these are susceptible to a number of pests and diseases. Watch out for caterpillars that may ruin foliage. Acid soils should be lightly limed before planting. Plants grow 20–25 cm high and should be spaced 30 cm apart so the shape and foliage are not distorted.
SEASON: Sow seed from autumn to early spring. In warmer regions autumn sowing is best. Plants should develop their full form and colour within 14–16 weeks of sowing.

Cabbage 'Ornamental Tokyo Mixed F1'

CALENDULA

The traditional pot marigold or English marigold is one of the easiest annuals to grow. Once only the plain orange species was available but today the many-petalled daisy-like flowers come in shades of yellow, orange, cream and honey. They are suitable for massed displays either alone or with other annuals and bulbs and make good container plants too. They make excellent cut flowers which last well if they are cut when the flowers are well formed but not fully open. Cutting flowers helps to extend the flowering period. Calendula can be grown in any type of well-drained soil but better growth and better flowers will result from soils enriched with compost or manure. They should be grown in full sun for best results. Space plants about 25 cm apart and closer in containers. Calendula rust is a fungal disease that sometimes attacks plants in humid, overcast conditions, especially if air circulation is poor.
SEASON: In warm zones seed should be sown in autumn to give a late winter and spring display. In cool regions seed should be sown at any time except during the winter months. From seed to flower will take approximately 10–12 weeks.

Calendula 'Greenheart Orange'

This is a most unusual variety of the pot marigold having rich orange flowers with a contrasting, quite distinctive green centre. The masses of petals give the flower a ruffled look. It makes a lovely garden flower and is very good for cutting. It is a tall grower, sometimes up to 60 cm high.

Calendula 'Pacific Beauty Mixed'

This is the more traditional calendula with large flowers in orange, lemon and cream. Popular with both adults and children alike, these plants are easy to grow and should reach a height of 50–60 cm. Grow 'Pacific Beauty Mixed' with blue cornflowers for contrast or use them to create an 'oranges and lemons' garden with Californian poppies and marigolds. These, too, make great cut flowers but they will give longer value if you leave them growing in the garden.

Calendula 'Pygmy Mixed'

This compact dwarf form of calendula is ideal for planting in pots or for growing at the front of flower beds as a border. The colour range is similar to other calendula strains as flowers are orange, cream and yellow but plants grow only to about 25 cm high. Their short stature makes them more suitable for exposed sites than their taller relatives. This easy-care plant is ideal for growing on balconies where conditions may be both windy and sunny. The flower stems are too short for floral arrangements but if spent flower heads are removed regularly the flowering period will be extended.

CALIFORNIAN POPPY

Guaranteed to bring cheer to any summer garden, Californian poppies can only be described as brilliant. Their single or double flowers have a satin sheen and the pretty foliage is grey-green and fern-like. The original species, which is the state flower of California, is vivid orange but there are other varieties that have flowers in shades of cream, yellow, bright red, rose and bronze. Flowers close at night and on very dull days but re-open the following day .Californian poppies must be grown in full sun, in soil that drains rapidly. They are not fussy as to soil type but they will not stand 'wet feet'. Difficult to transplant, they should be sown in the position where they are to grow. When

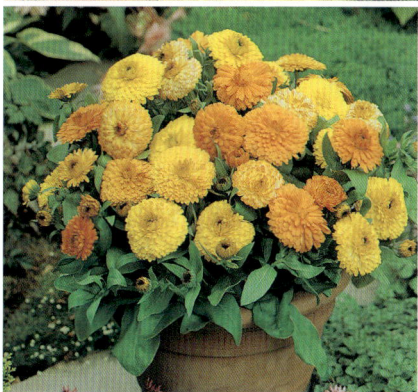

Top: Calendula 'Greenheart Orange'
Centre: 'Pacific Beauty Mixed'
Above: 'Pygmy Mixed'

Top left to right: Californian poppy 'Apricot Chiffon'; 'Mikado'
Above left to right: 'Prima Ballerina'; 'Single Mixed'

sowing it is best to mix the seed with sand and scatter it around, covering the seed only lightly. Plants can be carefully thinned out if necessary to 15 cm spacings. They look best when they are planted in drifts in the garden but also do well planted in pockets of a rockery. Although they are annuals, Californian poppies have a tendency to self-sow and turn up the following year in odd spots in the garden.

SEASON: Sow seed in spring or summer. Flowers should appear about 8 weeks after sowing.

Californian poppy 'Apricot Chiffon'
The silky petals of this rich apricot variety are prettily fluted. The reverse of the petals is a deeper coral pink in colour. Growing only about 25 cm high, this variety could be grown in a container or in the garden.

Californian poppy 'Mikado'
This lovely older variety has simple single flowers that are rich orange but scarlet on the reverse. The single flowers are quite lustrous against the finely divided leaves. It grows about 35 cm high.

Californian poppy 'Prima Ballerina'
This is a lovely selection, bearing double, frilled or fluted flowers in a wide range of colours. Colours range from soft pastels through to strong reds and oranges. Some flowers are two-toned. Growing only 25 cm high, it is a show-stopper.

Californian poppy 'Single Mixed'
Simple flowers such as this have great appeal for many gardeners. The lovely silky flowers range from bright red, through pinks and mauves to orange, cream and yellow. This strain grows taller than some, reaching 35 cm.

CAMPANULA 'CARPATICA BLUE'
This pretty, mound-forming perennial makes a good groundcover and is ideal for tucking into pockets of a rockery or retaining wall. Generally low growing, this plant may reach 30 cm in height and spread to 30–60 cm. It has rounded or heart-shaped leaves and produces masses of clear, soft blue flowers over many weeks in late spring or summer. Flowers are cup shaped and borne in such profusion as to obscure the foliage. Lightly prune after flowering to maintain the plant's good shape. It does best in slightly cooler areas. It will grow in sun in cool climates but generally prefers partial shade. Soil should drain well and contain plenty of organic matter. In warm areas it must be protected from strong wind and hot summer sun. Space plants about 25 cm apart.
SEASON: Sow seed from late summer to early spring. Seed sown in late summer or autumn should produce flowering plants the following summer.

CANDYTUFT 'FAIRY MIXED'
This easily grown annual produces compact, dome-shaped heads of flowers in soft shades of pink, lavender, crimson and white. Growing 25–30 cm high, it makes a pretty edging for a garden bed and also does well in pots. In the garden, space seedlings 20 cm apart but plant more closely in containers. This candytuft has a long flowering season from late spring through summer so seed may be sown over a few weeks to prolong the show. Seeds are best planted where they are to grow as they do not transplant easily. The flowers cut well and make very pretty posies. Their colours team well with stock, linaria and pinks. Grow in humus-rich soil that drains well. Dust soil with lime or dolomite prior to planting.
SEASON: Sow in autumn to early winter or in spring in cold districts. Flowers in 12–16 weeks.

Campanula 'Carpatica Blue'

Candytuft 'Fairy Mixed'

CANTERBURY BELLS 'CUP AND SAUCER'

An old-fashioned favourite, Canterbury bells grows to over 70 cm tall producing its large bell-shaped flowers right up the stems. The bell flower sits on its own little saucer giving rise to the name of this strain. Flowers in this mix include pink, blue, mauve and white shades. This is a classic plant for the cottage garden and should be massed to get the best effect. Although truly a biennial in cool climates, it is best treated as an annual in warm areas. It is not suitable for the tropics. Plants will grow in sun or partial shade but must have wind protection to avoid damage to the tall flower spikes. Space plants at about 30 cm intervals. Soil should drain well but contain enough organic matter to retain some moisture at all times.

SEASON: Sow seed in autumn. In warm zones plants should flower the next spring or early summer. In cool regions plants may spend the first spring and summer growing and developing to flower the following year.

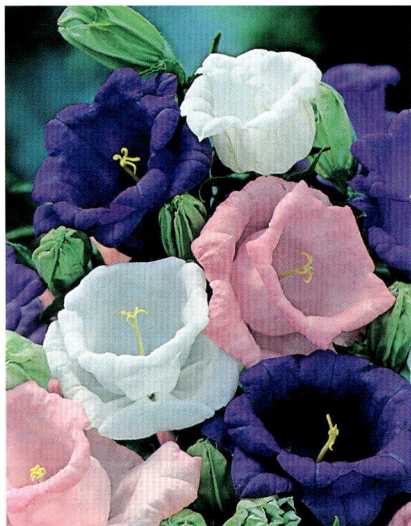

Canterbury Bells 'Cup and Saucer'

CARNATION

Carnations are said to be the most popular cut flower in the world. Certainly they are well loved as garden plants and will thrive as long as they are grown in full sun in very well drained soil. If there is any doubt about the drainage, grow them in pots or raised beds. They do best in climates where summers are hot and dry and may perform poorly in regions where summers are warm and wet. Rust, a fungal disease, may be a problem in warm, humid areas. Many carnations are

Top: Carnation 'Choice Double Mixed'
Above: 'Striped and Picotee Mixed'

delightfully fragrant and the colour range is wide. Their soft grey-green foliage sets off the flowers to perfection. Although many are classed as perennials, they tend to become rangy and sprawling after one growing season so the following annual selections should give great results. Thin canes can be inserted among the plants with string stretched between them to act as a discreet support for plants if they tend to flop.

SEASON: Spring and autumn are the best times for sowing seed but it can be planted year round. Plants will flower around 4–5 months after sowing.

Carnation 'Choice Double Mixed'
This is truly a mix of very choice flowers with a lovely colour range. Flowers range from white through pale to deep pink, scarlet and deep crimson, yellow and some streaked in contrasting colours. Many have the lovely clove scent associated with carnations. Growing about 45 cm tall, plants should be spaced 45 cm apart.

Carnation 'Striped and Picotee Mixed'
This lovely mix contains a great colour range with flowers that are flecked, striped or edged with contrasting colour. 'Picotee' describes a flower with a neat little edging of contrasting colour. These are great favourites as cut flowers as well as for garden display. They are nostalgic reminders of the pinks and carnations of former times as they resemble many of the older types that were worn as buttonholes and used in posies. These, however, grow to about 45 cm.

CELOSIA 'PRINCE OF WALES FEATHERS'
Also known as cockscomb or feathery amaranth, this striking annual produces bright plume-like flowers in strong colours. Flower colours include deep

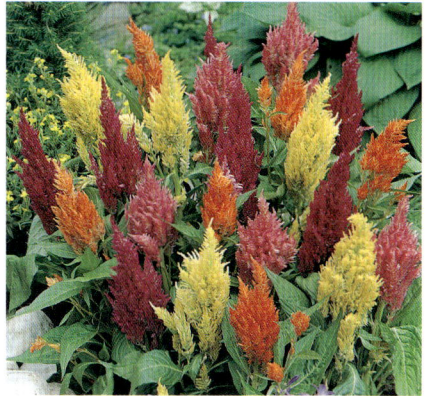
Celosia 'Prince of Wales Feathers'

scarlet and crimson, orange and yellow, all hot colours to add a tropical look to the summer garden. They should be grown massed on their own or teamed with other strong coloured flowers such as marigolds or gaillardias. Growing only about 30 cm high, they would make a vivid splash of colour in a container on a balcony. Plants should be spaced 20–30 cm apart in the garden, closer in containers. They need full sun and plenty of heat. Soil must drain well and should be enriched with organic matter to sustain plants over their long season. They are often planted in public gardens because of their long display, which may last through summer and autumn.

SEASON: Sow seed in spring to early summer. From seed to flowering takes about 4 months.

CINERARIA 'SPRING GLORY'
For those with rather shady gardens, cineraria is the answer to a glorious display of spring colour. This compact grower reaches about 25 cm in height, producing lovely rounded plants that are massed with richly coloured flowers. Flower colours include crimson, purple, royal blue, magenta, pink, lavender and white with many bicolours. Massed

Cineraria 'Spring Glory'

Cleome 'Colour Fountain'

displays in the garden can be spectacular but they can also be used to edge a shrub border. They make great potted plants too. Single plants in small pots can be tucked in among ferns or other greenery or they can be massed in larger pots or troughs. In the garden, space plants 25–30 cm apart. Cinerarias prefer shelter and some shade, especially through the middle of the day, and will not tolerate frost. Plant them in well-drained soil enriched with organic matter. In some regions they are attacked each season by a leafminer that damages the leaves but does not affect flowering. As this insect can only be controlled with systemic insecticides it is probably best to ignore it.
SEASON: Sow in late summer to autumn. Flowering-sized plants develop after about 5 months.

CLARKIA 'CHOICE DOUBLE MIXED'
See Godetia (pages 61–2).

CLEOME 'COLOUR FOUNTAIN'
These elegant annuals are tall growers reaching from 90 cm to 1.2 m or more in height. The light and airy flower heads appear over a very long period through summer and autumn, opening right up the stem as it grows taller. Long, fine whiskery stamens protrude way beyond the pink, white, rose, or lilac flowers. This tall plant is good for growing at the back of borders but also makes a fine accent plant when planted in groups around the garden. Grow in any kind of well-drained soil in full sun, preferably with protection from strong wind. Suitable for all but the coldest areas, seed should be sown where it is to grow in spring or early summer in cool regions. Sow seed thinly, removing the weaker plants later to allow spacings of 30–50 cm between plants.
SEASON: Sow in spring to early summer. Flowers should appear approximately 12 weeks after sowing.

COLEUS
Coleus is grown for its striking multi-coloured foliage. Also called flame nettle or painted leaves, it is popular as a potted plant grown indoors. Coleus can be grown in containers but makes a great filler plant between shrubs and adds texture and colour to bedding displays. It is a short-lived perennial best grown as

an annual. Growth is rapid and plants provide many months of colour. In cool climates it is often used in summer bedding to create a tropical effect. During the growing season pinch out the growing tips regularly to encourage bushiness. Blue to purple flowers appear in late summer but they should be pinched out as they add little to the plant and will halt foliage growth if left on. Coleus has no tolerance for cold. It is best grown in partial shade although it will take sun as long as there is plenty of soil moisture. Space plants 30 cm apart in the garden.

SEASON: Sow indoors at any time of year, just pressing the seed into the mix. In warm areas sow seed in late winter to early spring to obtain good sized plants in 12–16 weeks.

Coleus 'Black Dragon'

The rounded lobed leaves of this cultivar are deep burgundy, almost black, fading to a rich crimson in the centre. Popular as a potted specimen, this plant can add a touch of drama to the garden with its intense colour. It grows to approximately 45 cm high.

Coleus 'Flame Dancers'

This selection gives a wonderful range of leaf patterns and colours. Adding colour to the garden without flowers, this looks best planted in groups to give a lift to an otherwise green corner of ferns or palms. Crowded into a container, this variety provides a bright splash of colour indoors or out. Plants grow about 30 cm high.

COREOPSIS 'MAHOGANY MIDGET'

This very adaptable and easy-care plant will give you a summer-long display of deepest red flowers. Ideally planted in large drifts, this will grow only 25 cm high and so can be grown in exposed gardens as well as in containers. It will grow in any well-drained soil and needs plenty of sun for best results. The intense colour of the flowers makes this a good companion for other strong-coloured annuals such as zinnias, marigolds and salvias. Plant 15–20 cm apart to get a good cover. Seed sown where it is to grow will germinate quickly once the soil is warm. Plants develop quickly too.

SEASON: Sow seed in spring or early summer. Plants should reach flowering size in 12–16 weeks.

Left to right: Coleus 'Black Dragon; coleus 'Flame Dancers'; coreopsis 'Mahogany Midget'

CORNFLOWER

Cornflower blue is used to describe the
most intense shade of blue and the original
species of cornflower was predominantly
this colour, but there are now some other
lovely selections that will give you a
range of soft colours. Cornflowers are
best grown in full sun with some wind
protection. They must have free-draining
soil. These are a feature of traditional
cottage gardens but can be grown in
many other types of display. They
need to be mass planted for best effect.
In a large garden the three selections
described below could be mixed for a
brilliant effect, the tall blue ones being
planted at the back. The main flowering
is middle to late spring through early
summer. They make excellent cut flowers.
SEASON: Sow through autumn into early
winter. Seedlings reach flowering size
in about 12 weeks. In cold areas sow in
late winter to early spring.

Cornflower 'Blue Ball'

This is the traditional blue cornflower
reminiscent of meadows and cottage
gardens. These plants grow up to 75 cm
high and should be spaced about
25 cm apart.

Cornflower 'Frosty'

All the flowers in this range are edged
with white, which gives them this name.
Soft blue, pink, maroon and white with
darker centres make up this pretty
selection. They grow 40 to 60 cm high
and should be planted about 25 cm apart.

Cornflower 'Polka Dot'

This pretty, low-growing cornflower could
be happily grown in pots. As it grows only
30–45 cm high, the effect of a massed
planting would be most decorative. In the
garden, space plants at 20–25 cm
intervals but close plant in containers. A
feature of this selection is that most
flowers have distinctive dark centres.

COSMEA

Cosmea is another name for cosmos,
both words deriving from the Greek
kosmos meaning beautiful. Few annuals can
beat cosmeas for their long flowering and
decorative value in the garden and as cut
flowers. Dead-head regularly and you will
have flowers through summer and well
into autumn. All are easy to grow. They
are tall growers and so should be planted
at the back of garden beds or the centre
of a circular bed. Foliage is fine and

Left to right: Cornflower 'Blue Ball'; 'Frosty'; 'Polka Dot'

Above left to right: Cosmea 'Bright Lights';
'Seashells Mixed', 'Sensation Mixed'
Below left: 'Sonata Mixed'

feathery, complementing the large, colourful flowers. These plants need full sun and protection from strong wind. They will grow in any type of well-drained soil. Plant seeds about 30 cm apart. Plant growth is rapid once the soil warms and days are long. In cool zones delay planting until conditions warm, as these plants are very frost tender.
SEASON: Sow in spring through summer where they are to grow. It takes about 16 weeks from seed to flowering.

Cosmea 'Bright Lights'

This is the only mix of cosmea containing strong, clear red, yellow and orange flowers. Colours blend in well with dahlias and red salvias for a hot summer look. Plants grow from 60 cm to 1 m.

Cosmea 'Seashells Mixed'

This selection has mostly softly coloured flowers with fluted, rolled petals. Flowers are quite unusual and range through pink, cream or white, and crimson. These grow to 90 cm high.

Cosmea 'Sensation Mixed'

This is a mix of very large single flowers in pinks, white or reds. Flowers may be 9 cm or more across. Plants grow to 90 cm or more, and flower for months if you keep picking them or dead-heading.

Cosmea 'Sonata Mixed'

The Sonata strain of cosmea tends to be more compact in growth. Plants rarely exceed 50–60 cm in height, making them more suitable for exposed sites than taller forms. Flowers are mainly in strong pink or cerise tones with some white or deeper red flowers. Foliage is fine and almost fluffy looking, providing a pretty background for lower growing plants.

COSMIDIUM 'BRUNETTE'

This very unusual annual creates a striking effect in the garden and makes a lovely cut flower. It is enjoying a revival of interest as it is known to have been in cultivation since the nineteenth century. The deep mahogany-brown flowers have a wide yellow edge, creating a feathered effect on the petals. Growing 45 cm high, it enjoys the same conditions as cosmea and cosmos, namely a position in full sun and light well-drained soil. For a gold, orange and brown border it teams well with marigolds and 'Mahogany Midget' coreopsis, which have similar tonings. It could also be grown with Cosmea 'Bright Lights'. Seed can be sown where it is to grow and the seedlings later thinned to 30 cm spacings.

SEASON: Sow seed in spring through summer. Plants take about 16 weeks to reach flowering size.

COSMOS 'PURITY'

White flowers add a cool look to the summer garden and none better than this. Even at night they add something special to the garden. The simple flowers are pure white and borne in great profusion among the feathery leaves. Growing to

Cosmidium 'Brunette'

Cosmos 'Purity'

90 cm, this plant makes a good backdrop to other, lower growing annuals and perennials. It should have protection from strong wind and be grown in full sun. Plant seeds about 30 cm apart. It can be grown in any type of well-drained soil, flowering throughout summer and autumn as long as spent flowers are removed regularly. It makes a good cut flower, especially if flowers are cut when they first open.

SEASON: Sow seed in spring through summer. Plants mature to flowering size in about 16 weeks.

DAHLIA

Dahlias are perennials and are often grown from tuberous roots, but bedding dahlias are very easy and rewarding to grow from seed. They are quick growing and with regular picking or dead-heading will give flowers over many weeks of summer and autumn. Like all dahlias they are heavy feeders and will do best in well-drained soil that has been heavily enriched with manure or compost two or three weeks before planting. They need full sun all day for good flowering and plenty of water through summer. There is a great range of flower colour and flower

Left to right: Dahlia 'Dwarf Double Mixed'; 'Pompom Mixed'; 'Rigoletto'

form to add interest to the garden as well as to provide a supply of cut flowers. Dahlias are a magnet for snails and grasshoppers that will chew both leaves and flowers, so you should keep watch for these pests. Although there are a number of diseases that can attack dahlias, the bedding types are often less susceptible.

SEASON: Seed is sown in spring to early summer. Plants should flower about 16–20 weeks later.

Dahlia 'Dwarf Double Mixed'

This seed selection gives masses of colour in the garden during the summer and autumn months and plenty of cut flowers for the house. Flowers are brightly coloured, the range including red, yellow, pink, white and russet. Growing 60 cm high, plants need protection from the wind. Plants should be spaced about 30 cm apart.

Dahlia 'Pompon Mixed'

The small rounded flower heads of pompon dahlias have great appeal. Flowers are quite circular with the massed petals being rolled and curved to create a honeycomb effect. There may be just a

few seedlings that do not come true to type but these will still provide garden colour. Flowers are long lasting and great for picking. The colour range includes various shades of red and pink, yellow and cerise to lilac. This is a tall grower to around 90 cm and so needs shelter from wind. It may need staking.

Dahlia 'Rigoletto'

This is possibly the most versatile of all the bedding dahlias as it will grow only 40 cm high while still producing a great floral display. The great colour range includes bright red, yellow, orange, pink and white. Because of its neat stature it can be grown in containers, making it ideal for growing on balconies and terraces as well as in the garden. With care and regular cutting these will provide decoration for weeks and weeks.

SOWING FINE SEED

A good way of sowing tiny seeds is to mix them with a little fine dry sand. Scatter this thinly over the surface of moist seed-raising mixture.

DAISY 'ENGLISH MIXED'

These mixed fully double flowers are large and pompon-like, ranging from deep red through pinks to white. They flower through spring into early summer, later in cool areas. Plants grow only about 15 cm high with a similar spread, making this an ideal plant for gardens. Although truly a perennial, this is best grown as an annual. Plants should be grown in full sun but will take some shade. They will grow in most soils but mulching plants conserves root moisture in dry springs. Space plants 10–15 cm apart in the garden, closer in containers.
SEASON: Sow seed from autumn to early spring. Plants take 12–14 weeks to reach flowering size.

DELPHINIUM

A mainstay of mixed borders and cottage gardens, delphiniums are perennials most often grown as annuals in warm climates. They are known for their range of rich blue flowers but some mixes now contain pink, white, cream and lavender to purple shades. Generally fast growing, delphiniums give a long flowering display in the garden and make good cut flowers. Most are tall growers needing wind

protection. They do best in full sun in well-drained soil that is enriched with organic matter and plenty of water during the growing season.
SEASON: In warm zones sow late summer through autumn. In cool zones sow in spring or under cover in autumn. From seed to flower takes about 20 weeks.

Delphinium 'Blue Cloud'

The soft blue flowers in this mix are loosely arranged on stems up to 75 cm in height. In the garden, space 30–40 cm apart. Plants will flower in spring and/or summer depending on district.

Delphinium 'Pacific Giant Mixed'

These stately plants grow from 1.5 to 2 m and should be planted at the back of beds. They may also be used as accent plants. Plants may need staking with light canes. The stiff flower spikes are made up of numerous semi-double individual blooms of blue, purple, lavender, lilac, pink and white. Space plants 45 cm apart.

DIANTHUS

Most of these members of the carnation family are really short-lived perennials

Left to right: Daisy 'English Mixed'; delphinium 'Blue Cloud'; delphinium 'Pacific Giant Mixed'

but are best treated as annuals in all but cool climates. These short, tufty plants bear single or double flowers, mainly in white, pink and red shades. Very few have perfume. They are quite fast growing and flower through spring and summer in cool areas, spring only in warm zones. Grow in full sun in very free-draining soil to which lime has been added.

SEASON: Sow in autumn or spring. Plants flower 14–16 weeks after sowing.

Dianthus 'Baby Doll Mixed'

This neat plant grows only 15 cm high. Many of the single pink, red or white

flowers in this mix have a contrasting darker eye. Plant seedlings 15 cm apart.

Dianthus 'Double Gaiety Mixed'

This mix produces unusual double flowers that have fringed, ragged petals. Flowers are scented and come in many shades of pink, red, salmon and white. Plants grow about 30 cm high and so should be spaced at least 25 cm apart.

Dianthus 'Merry-Go-Round'

These neat little plants grow about 20 cm high, spreading about the same width. The single flowers are pure white with a rich red eye. It makes a pretty show in the garden or massed in troughs.

Pink 'Old Fashioned Mixed'

Pinks are *Dianthus* species and this mix contains some of the old-fashioned pinks that look and smell delicious. This mix is part of the Granny's Garden range, and while they are cottage garden plants they also suit tubs and troughs. Heights may vary but are generally around 30 cm. The pretty fringed flowers include singles and doubles in shades of pink, soft crimson and white. Many have contrasting centres. Space plants about 15 cm apart.

Top left: Dianthus 'Baby Doll Mixed'. Above left to right: Dianthus 'Double Gaiety Mixed'; dianthus 'Merry-Go-Round'; pink 'Old Fashioned Mixed'

DIASCIA 'PINK QUEEN'

This annual type of diascia has a slightly trailing habit, making it just right for hanging baskets, troughs or for the edges of garden walls. In mild areas plants may keep growing for two years. Soft pink flowers grow right up the stems, appearing over many weeks in late spring and summer. When cut back after the first flush it will often produce another good show. Plants grow around 30 cm high but will not stand up straight. Space about 20 cm apart. They need sun for at least half a day and do best in rich soil that drains well.

SEASON: Seed is best sown in autumn or spring. Plants take 18–20 weeks from seed to flower.

DIMORPHOTHECA 'NEW HYBRIDS'

This is one of the colourful African daisies that bring sunshine to the garden with its bright flowers in yellow, orange, rich cream and white. Plant this in the hottest spot in the garden in well-drained soil and you will have a lovely show right through summer. Plants grow about 30 cm high and should be spaced about 40 cm apart. To gain the maximum impact from these plants grow them in broad sweeps. They can be grown as annual groundcover, especially on sloping banks where the soil is rather dry. Flowers cut well but will give better value in the garden, especially if dead flowers are removed regularly.

SEASON: Sow from early spring to early summer. These can be planted directly where they are to grow. It takes 12–16 weeks from seed to flowering.

ERIGERON 'PROFUSION'

Masses of tiny starry daisies cover this dainty plant for months on end. The slender stems grow 20–30 cm high but are lax and spreading, carrying their small pink or white flowers. This is often grown as a groundcover, to fill spaces in paving or in pots and hanging baskets. For quick cover space plants 15 cm apart. Strictly speaking, this is a creeping perennial but this selection is best grown as an annual. It is tough and easy to grow in any well-drained soil but needs full sun for at least half a day. Plants have a tendency to self-seed in warm climates. Cut back after the first flowering to keep plants compact.

SEASON: Sow seed in late summer through autumn in mild areas, in spring in cool zones. Plants take 16 weeks or more from seed to flower.

Left to right: Diascia 'Pink Queen'; dimorphotheca 'New Hybrids'; erigeron 'Profusion'

Left to right: Forget-me-not 'Indigo'; foxglove 'Excelsior Hybrids'; gaillardia 'Grandiflora Mixed'

FORGET-ME-NOT 'INDIGO'

When grown in light shade under trees, forget-me-nots create carpets of deep blue for weeks on end. These well-loved annuals tend to self-seed. They are the easiest of plants to grow, needing only soil that retains a little moisture and shade through the hottest part of the day. They may grow 20–30 cm high and so should be spaced around 15 cm apart. They look lovely in posies and last quite well when cut. Plant them among other spring-flowering annuals or bulbs to get a delightful effect.

SEASON: Sow seeds from late summer through autumn. From seed to flower takes about 12 weeks.

FOXGLOVE 'EXCELSIOR HYBRIDS'

Another delightful plant for the cottage garden, foxgloves are grown as biennials or perennials depending on climate. Tall spires of flowers rise from a rosette of grey-green, slightly furry leaves. Flower spikes, which may be up to 1.5 m tall, are long lasting in the garden and make good cut flowers. The long spires are made up of numerous bell-shaped flowers in white, cream, pink and purple, each with a heavily spotted throat. They can be grown in the sun in cool climates but are best in dappled sunlight or shade. They need shelter from strong wind to avoid toppling the tall flowers. Soil should be enriched with organic matter before planting. They need plenty of water in dry or windy conditions. Gardeners should take careful note that all parts of this plant are poisonous.

SEASON: Sow in late summer or autumn, thinning seedlings so that plants are spaced 30 cm apart. Plants take 10–12 weeks from seed to flowering

GAILLARDIA 'GRANDIFLORA MIXED'

Known as Indian blanket or blanket flower, this is an easy-to-grow plant, thriving even in poor soils. The large daisy-type flowers are vividly coloured in tones of red, yellow, orange and mahogany. They give a long garden display through late spring and summer and also cut well. This hardy perennial grows 75 cm high and looks well with low-growing gazanias in the same colour range. Both enjoy hot sites in full sun. Seed can be sown directly where it is to grow and thinned to 30 cm spacings.

SEASON: Sow seed in autumn or in spring in cool districts. Plants take from 16 to 20 weeks from seed to flower.

Gazania 'Sunshine Hybrids'

Geranium 'Matisse F2'

GAZANIA 'SUNSHINE HYBRIDS'

This very colourful perennial makes a great groundcover, providing flowers over a very long period through spring and summer. Flowering can be prolonged by regular dead-heading. There is a brilliant colour range from soft pinks and cream through to yellow, orange, deep mahogany and red, all with contrasting centres. There are some attractive bicolours too. This is a good soil binder and can be used to hold soil on banks or to stop sand drift in seaside locations. It also makes a good edging plant and is ideal for containers in exposed sunny positions. It must be grown in full sun in well-drained soil to do well. Individual plants may in time spread 30 cm or more and so should be spaced at about 25 cm intervals. Flowers are unsuitable for cutting.
SEASON: Sow seed in spring or early summer. Plants take about 12 weeks from seed to flower.

GERANIUM 'MATISSE F2'

Most gardeners think of growing geraniums from cuttings but they can be most successfully raised from seed. As well as being old garden favourites, these perennial geraniums are very popular pot plants. This lovely selection includes flowers in colours of rose-pink, scarlet, white and salmon and possibly some bicolours. Sturdy plants grow around 40 cm high and some may have dark zoning on their scalloped leaves. Geraniums must be grown in full sun all day in very free-draining soil. Space plants 20–30 cm apart. Add a little lime or dolomite to the soil before planting seedlings in their permanent positions. While growing seedlings need regular water, established plants can be allowed to dry out between waterings. In humid coastal areas geraniums are often attacked by fungal rust.
SEASON: In warm areas sow seed from late winter through spring. In cool zones sow in spring through summer. Time from seed to flower varies greatly but will be about 20 weeks.

SOWING GERANIUM SEEDS

I get best results by sowing the geranium seeds on edge and keeping soil temperature at about 20°C day and night. At the first sign of growth, move the seedling box to a slightly cooler spot where night temperature is about 15°C.

GERBERA 'AFRICAN DAISY'

Gerberas are perennials that may be best treated as annuals unless conditions are ideal. However as plants take several months to reach maturity, seeds would have to be raised in a glasshouse over winter to achieve this. Also known as Transvaal daisies, these single or semi-double gerberas produce brightly coloured flowers in a range that includes salmon, red, yellow, orange and white. They look best planted in groups in the garden. They also do well in pots and as they must have perfect drainage this may be the best option for those gardening on clay. Gerberas also need full sun and protection from strong wind. Flowers cut well for the vase and it is essential to remove spent flowers from plants to keep them blooming over a long season. With regular attention they can be in flower from late spring through until autumn. These plants grow about 60 cm high and should be spaced about 40 cm apart. Take care when transplanting seedlings to keep the crown above soil level. Rust and fungal leaf spots may be a problem in very humid conditions.

SEASON: Sow seed in spring through early summer. Plants take from 30 to 40 weeks to reach flowering size.

Gerbera 'African Daisy'

Geum 'Mrs. Bradshaw'

GEUM 'MRS. BRADSHAW'

This bright scarlet perennial is an old favourite for growing in mixed borders or among shrubs. It looks best when planted in groups as its fiery colour will make a strong feature in the garden. Growing from 40 to 60 cm high, flowers stand well clear of rosettes of pretty lobed leaves that have a slightly hairy texture. Geum is best grown in full sun in cool districts but prefers afternoon shade in warmer areas. The flowers are not really suitable for cutting. Plants should bloom throughout late spring and summer if you remove the spent flowers regularly. This plant needs well-drained soil that has been enriched with organic matter. Space plants about 30 cm apart and mulch them to conserve moisture.

SEASON: Sow seed in autumn or spring. Plants will take 16 weeks from seed to flowering.

GODETIA

Godetias are also known as farewell to spring or clarkia. They are the last of the spring-flowering annuals to come into bloom, bridging the gap between spring and summer displays. The open, cup-shaped flowers are prettily ruffled and in shades of red, pink, white and lavender.

From left to right: Godetia 'Dwarf Mixed'; godetia 'Salmon Princess'; clarkia 'Choice Double Mixed'

Plants vary in height and can be planted in drifts or in containers. Flowering in middle to late spring in warm areas, the display will continue into summer in cool regions. They need an open, sunny position and will grow in any well-drained soil.

SEASON: Sow in autumn to early winter in frost-free areas or in spring, ideally where it is to grow. Plants take 12–14 weeks from seed to flowering.

Godetia 'Dwarf Mixed'

This pretty selection grows only 25 cm high and so is ideal for the front of garden beds and shrub borders. It also looks lovely massed in pots or troughs. It has a lovely colour range with many two-toned flowers and is excellent as a cut flower. Space plants 20 cm apart in the ground, closer in pots.

Godetia 'Salmon Princess'

The rich salmon-pink flowers of this variety are frilled or ruffled. While they can be teamed with other pastel flowers they do make a lovely show on their own. Plants grow only 30 cm high and so can also look attractive in containers. Space plants about 25 cm apart.

Clarkia 'Choice Double Mixed'

The ruffled flowers in this mix come in a range of colours that includes red, pink, white and lavender to purple. Plants will grow up to 45 cm high but they are narrow and can be close planted at 15 cm intervals. Protect plants from strong wind as they may be rather top heavy in flower and are inclined to blow over. Light canes interwoven with string can be placed among plants. This lovely garden plant is also excellent for cutting.

GOURD 'ORNAMENTAL MIXED'

Ornamental gourds are included with the flowering plants even though they are cultivated for their fruit rather than their flower. The fruit is popular for indoor decoration when dried and displayed in bowls or baskets. Gourds come in an amazing range of shapes, colours and markings and are popular with both children and adults. They grow on vines that are best supported by lattice, wire or trellis. They can be allowed to trail along the ground but flowers and fruit of vines grown on the ground are very susceptible to snail attack. Grow in full sun in rich soil with a plentiful water supply during the growing season. Space the plants

Gourd 'Ornamental Mixed'

GYPSOPHILA

With its billowing masses of small flowers gypsophila is widely used as a cut flower and adds an airy touch to other, heavier textured flowers. It is often known as baby's breath. These annual varieties are quick growing and can be sown over several weeks to ensure a succession of flowers. Gypsophila can be planted in drifts to create the illusion of a meadow or as a foil for other flowering annuals or bulbs. It does best when grown in full sun but it will tolerate any kind of soil as long as it drains well. Space the plants about 15 cm apart. Gypsophila does best in cooler climates and is unsuitable for hot, arid or tropical regions. It is quite cold and frost hardy.

SEASON: You can sow seed any time of the year except midsummer or midwinter. The flowers appear about 10 weeks after seed is sown.

Gypsophila 'Bright Rose'

Growing from 45 to 60 cm high, this finely branched annual produces bright rose-pink flowers. It is lovely planted in drifts in the garden and is also an excellent plant for cutting and for use in bouquets.

40–50 cm apart. The fruit should not be eaten and is best left to ripen fully on the vine until quite hard. Cut ripe fruit with a short length of stem attached and allow it to dry in a warm, dry place for several weeks. Dry fruit can then be given a coat of clear varnish to preserve its colours.

SEASON: Sow seed where it is to grow in late spring to early summer. From seed to fruit takes 16–20 weeks.

Left to right: Gypsophila 'Bright Rose'; 'Monarch White'; 'Snow Fountain'

Gypsophila 'Monarch White'

The tiny white flowers of this variety are very popular for floral work as even a tiny sprig adds a dainty touch to other, more solid flowers. This grows 45 cm high and is a good companion for carnations and pinks.

Gypsophila 'Snow Fountain'

This variety has extra large, pure white flowers on plants growing to 45 cm. Plants have strong upright growth with sturdy stems that make it especially good for cutting.

HELICHRYSUM 'DRAKKAR PASTEL MIXTURE'

This mix is from the Flower Arrangers range. Everlastings, paper daisies and strawflowers are some of the names applied to these attractive flowers. You can enjoy them in the garden—where they will grow about 75 cm high—and then harvest the flowers for drying. However, you should note that flowers for drying must be picked when the petals are well formed but still incurved. The flowers are then tied in bunches and hung upside down in a dry, airy place to complete the drying process. This mix contains shades of pink, salmon, cream, yellow and orange. Plants must be grown

Helichrysum 'Drakkar Pastel Mixture'

in full sun in very quick-draining soil. The soil does not need to be rich; in fact these plants will grow better in sandy or gravelly soils. Space plants 30 cm apart. SEASON: Sow in autumn or early winter in warm areas or in spring in cooler regions. Plants take roughly 16 weeks from seed to flower.

HELIPTERUM 'ROSEUM SPECIAL MIXED'

See Strawflower (pages 91–2).

HOLLYHOCK

This is a true perennial in cool climates but may be best grown as an annual in warmer areas although plants tend to bloom more prolifically in their second year. Summer is the peak season for hollyhocks. Grow hollyhocks in full sun but with protection from wind that may topple the tall plants. Plants may need staking if the site is not sheltered. Hollyhocks prefer a soil that has been enriched with organic matter. Space the plants about 30 cm apart. SEASON: Sow in late summer to autumn for flowers the following summer or in early spring. Spring-sown plants grow rapidly and should flower in late summer or early autumn.

Hollyhock 'Chaters Double Mixed'

This unusual mix of hollyhocks will surprise many who are familiar with the pinks and purples of the more traditional range. This selection produces double peony form flowers in really striking colours of red, yellow, burgundy, white and bright pink. Flowers are heavily ruffled and tightly packed onto the tall stems that may grow up to 2 m high.

Hollyhock 'Giant Single Mixed Colours'

This is the original cottage garden hollyhock and it is included in the Granny's Garden range.

Top: Hollyhock 'Chaters Double Mixed'
Above: 'Giant Single Mixed Colours'

SOLVING SHADE PROBLEMS

Some flowering annuals do well in the shade, especially those that flower in late winter and spring. These include primula, polyanthus, cineraria, Canterbury bells, impatiens and aquilegia. Foxgloves, lobelia and mimulus can be grown in shade too. Pansy, viola, alyssum and wallflower will tolerate partial shade.

HONESTY 'PURPLE AND WHITE MIXED'

Although the purple and white flowers of this plant are decorative in the spring garden, honesty is most often grown for its circular, smooth, silvery pods that are highly sought after for dried arrangements. The seeds are in fact part of Mr. Fothergill's Flower Arrangers range. Honesty is quite a tough plant that will grow in sun or partial shade in almost any type of soil that drains well. Partial shade is a must in warmer areas. Plants grow from 45 to 60 cm high and should be spaced about 30 cm apart. Although the flowers can be cut for the vase, most gardeners prefer to leave these to mature on the plant. You should cut the pods when they are mature and dry; they are usually in this condition by late summer or autumn. Hang bunches upside down in a dry, airy place until you are able to carefully remove the outer skin of the pod to reveal the silvery lining.

SEASON: Sow in autumn or spring. Plants should flower about 12 weeks after sowing.

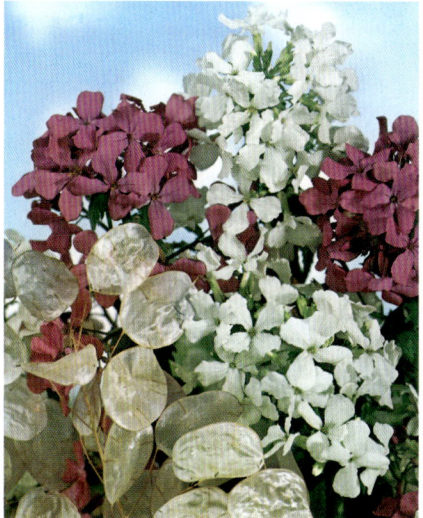

Honesty 'Purple and White Mixed'

IMPATIENS

Busy Lizzies or impatiens have to be one of the easiest and most rewarding of plants to grow. These perennials will flower for most of the year, providing brilliant colour in partial shade. They grow beautifully in pots and hanging baskets as well as in the garden. They do like moisture but not poor drainage. Their colours are bright and cheerful, guaranteed to lift the spirits. If plants are cut back after flowers have faded they will continue to bloom. However, they don't like cold so in cool climates they must be either grown as annuals or given warmth and shelter through winter. SEASON: In warm climates sow any time of year except midwinter and midsummer. In cool climates sow in spring. Plants take about 12 weeks from seed to flowering.

Impatiens 'Safari Mixed F2'

Growing about 30 cm high, the plants in this mix produce single flowers in white and clear, strong scarlet and pink. For massed displays you should space plants about 25 cm apart.

Impatiens 'Starbright Mixed F1'

All the flowers in this mix are brightly coloured, each featuring a central white star. Flowers in this mix come in colours including red, rose-pink, orange and violet. Growing to only 20 cm high, this plant makes a pretty border and is ideal for growing in pots. Space plants about 20 cm apart for full cover.

Impatiens 'Super Elfin Mixed F1'

Also growing about 20 cm high, plants in this selection tend to have a slightly spreading habit. Flowers come in numerous shades of red, pink, white, orange and salmon with a few bicolours. This is probably the best of the dwarf varieties for the garden or containers.

Top: Impatiens 'Safari Mixed F2'
Centre: 'Starbright Mixed F1'
Above: 'Super Elfin Mixed F1'

LARKSPUR

Also known as sweet rocket, the annual larkspurs are close relatives of delphiniums but do not grow as tall. For smaller gardens where delphiniums may be overpowering these will take their place. They have pretty, fern-like foliage and carry densely packed spires of flowers in spring or early summer. They are perfect for cottage gardens or for blending with other annuals and bulbs in pastel colours. They will grow in sun or partial shade but need wind protection. Soil should drain well but have a high organic content. Flowers last longer in cool climates where they flower in summer. In warmer areas they flower in spring. However, they are unsuitable for tropical gardens.

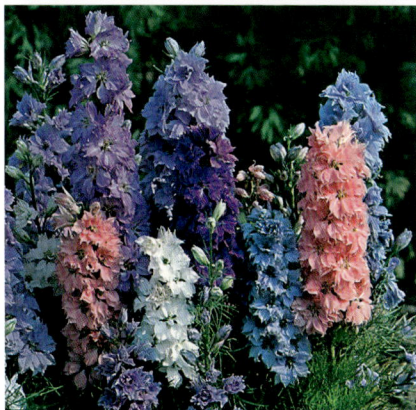

SEASON: Sow in autumn or early winter, also in spring in cool districts. Plants take 20 weeks from seed to flower.

Larkspur 'Giant Imperial Mixed'

Growing about 90 cm tall this selection branches from the base carrying masses of double flowers on strong stems. This is good for garden display but especially good for cut flowers. In cool to mild climates the floral display may last for 8–10 weeks. Colours range from rich purple, through lavender, pale and rose-pink and white. Space plants 30 cm apart.

Larkspur 'Hyacinth Dwarf Mixed'

Plants in this series grow only about 50 cm high and do not branch from the base. However, the colour range is similar to that of the taller 'Giant Imperial'. The flowering spikes are densely packed with double flowers also lasting well in cool regions. They are pretty in the garden or cut for the vase.

LAVATERA

These striking annuals should be grown more often as they flower over a long period and are quite easy to grow. Almost shrub-like, they are known as rose mallow or tree mallow. They have attractive lobed leaves and their large silky flowers are an open cup shape. Although they can be cut for indoors you will get better value by leaving them in the garden. They can be the dominant feature of a garden display or used as background planting for smaller annuals and perennials. All are best grown in full sun in any moderately rich soil that drains well. Final spacings should be 40 cm apart.

SEASON: Sow in autumn in warm zones and in spring to early summer in cool zones. Autumn-sown plants flower in late spring to early summer; spring-sown plants flower through summer to early autumn.

Top: Larkspur 'Giant Imperial Mixed'
Above: 'Hyacinth Dwarf Mixed'

Left to right: Lavatera 'Mont Blanc'; 'Parade Mixed'; 'Silver Cup'

Lavatera 'Mont Blanc'

Growing 50–60 cm high, this lovely plant bears its pure white flowers right through summer. White flowers can be teamed with any other colour but these would look particularly stunning with white cosmos or white cleome, and bordered by white alyssum to create an all-white display.

Lavatera 'Parade Mixed'

This is an exceptionally pretty mix of pink and white flowers. The pink flowers are veined in darker tones to add to the decorative effect. Growing 60 cm high, a planting of this selection will give you a lovely garden display when used alone or with other plants.

Lavatera 'Silver Cup'

Flowers of this cultivar are described as silvery pink or rose-pink in colour. The open, satiny flowers are veined in deeper tones, adding greatly to the beauty of the plant. This would make a lovely feature either mass planted or planted at the centre of a garden bed surrounded by other smaller flowering annuals in complementary tones. It will grow about 60 cm high.

LAVENDER 'ENGLISH DWARF'

Never out of fashion, lavender is a must for any sunny garden. This dwarf form, growing to 30 cm, can be used for low hedging or as a potted plant or it can simply be added to garden beds of mixed perennials, annuals and small shrubs. Flowers can be used fresh in posies or gathered and dried to make sachets or add to potpourris. Foliage is grey-green and highly aromatic and is topped by spikes of blue-lavender flowers. This quick-growing perennial must be grown

Lavender 'English Dwarf'

in sharply drained soil in full sun. Acid soils should be limed before planting. For hedging, space plants 15–20 cm apart. After flowering give an overall shearing as this will give more compact growth.
SEASON: Sow in autumn or early winter. Germination may be slow. Some flowers should appear the following spring and summer.

LINARIA 'FAIRY BOUQUET'

The dainty little flowers of linaria are like tiny snapdragons. The 'Fairy Bouquet' range has flowers in yellow, pink and purple, salmon, orange and white. This small grower, to 20 cm, must be planted in generous drifts to be effective. It looks lovely as a garden border and makes a good container plant. Space plants 5–8 cm apart and crowd them into containers to produce a good show. It will grow in full sun in well-drained soil, preferably enriched with manure or compost. This plant can be used as a cut flower but gives better value in the garden. If plants are cut back after flowering you should get a second blooming.
SEASON: Sow in autumn in warm zones, spring in cool areas. Plants take about 10 weeks from sowing to flowering.

Linaria 'Fairy Bouquet'

LOBELIA

Annual lobelias make ideal edging for garden beds and do equally well in pots, troughs, window boxes and hanging baskets. In warm areas they flower from late winter through spring, often into early summer. In cool zones they flower mainly in summer. They can be grown in full sun or partial shade and prefer a well-drained soil enriched with organic matter. They are quick growers that have a long flowering display. They are possibly best known for the intensity of their blue varieties but there are many others to choose from. If plants are clipped over after the first flowering they will often bloom again. They do best in warm climates as they are tolerant of only the lightest frosts.
SEASON: Sow in late summer or autumn in warm districts, spring in cool areas. Mix the fine seed with sand before sowing. Flowers appear about 12 weeks after sowing.

Lobelia 'Cascade Mixed'

This is a dainty trailing plant that is ideal for hanging baskets and tubs. Flowers are in shades of blue, mauve, white and pink to red. Space plants about 10 cm apart for an abundant show.

Lobelia 'Crystal Palace'

This little plant produces the most intense blue flowers against a background of slightly bronze foliage. This is the perfect edging plant as each plant forms a mound 10–15 cm high. A continuous ribbon of blue will be achieved if plants are spaced 8–10 cm apart.

Lobelia 'Sapphire' (trailing)

Blue flowers with a white eye are a feature of this trailing lobelia. This is another beauty for hanging baskets, troughs or low garden walls and rockeries. Plants can be spaced 8–10 cm apart for a very full effect.

Lobelia 'String of Pearls'

This mix produces a multi-coloured effect with flowers of blue, mauve, pink and white. It is most effective planted as a filler or groundcover where its mixed colours can be enjoyed. It is also used for edging. Plants should be spaced at 10–15 cm intervals.

Lobelia 'White Fountain'

The pure white flowers of this cascading variety will complement flowers of any other colour. In baskets or tubs it could be planted around bright geraniums or pastel-coloured godetias. There is really no limit to the potential uses of this lovely plant. You should space plants 8–10 cm apart.

SOWING IN DRILLS

It is traditional to sow annuals by broadcasting seed where it is to grow, but a surer method is to sow seed in oval or circular drills. You will get a more even display and it will be easier to spot the weeds.

Top left to right: Lobelia 'Cascade Mixed', 'Crystal Palace', 'Sapphire'
Above left to right: 'String of Pearls', 'White Fountain'

LUPIN 'RUSSELL MIXED'

Russell lupins are among the stars of the perennial border in late spring and early summer to midsummer. Suitable for cool climates only, plants can grow up to 1 m high, producing tall, densely packed spires of flowers in a myriad of colours. Flowers rise high above the pretty lobed leaves. In cool climates plants may produce several flower spikes per plant whereas in warm areas only one spike may be carried and plants must be treated as annuals. These plants can be grown in full sun or semi-shade but they must have wind protection. The soil need not be rich but it should drain well. Space plants 30 cm apart. Flowers can be cut for indoor decoration but will give better value in the garden. Seed should be soaked in some warm water for at least 12 hours before planting.

SEASON: Seed should be sown in late summer to autumn to bloom late in the following spring or early summer.

Lupin 'Russell Mixed'

LYCHNIS 'MALTESE CROSS'

The distinctive petal arrangement of its flattish scarlet flowers has given this bright plant the name of Maltese cross,

Lychnis 'Maltese Cross'

which it is thought to resemble. This quick-growing perennial flowers on stems 60 cm high. Established plants will flower year after year in late spring through early summer. It grows best in full sun but will tolerate shade for part of the day. It thrives in almost any kind of well-drained soil. Remove spent flowers as they fade to prolong the flowering period. Although it makes a good cut flower, it will probably last longer as part of the garden display. Space seedlings about 25 cm apart.

SEASON: Sow in autumn to early winter for flowers the following spring or summer.

MARIGOLD

Marigolds are easy to grow and reward the gardener with a very long flowering display. The many varieties all have flowers that are in shades of yellow, orange and deep red. They are broadly divided into French or African strains. French marigolds are available in much greater variety than African types. There is a great range in plant height and habit so they have a multitude of uses in the

Top left to right: Marigold 'Boy-O-Boy Mixed', 'Crackerjack', 'Dwarf Double Mixed'
Above left to right: 'Honeycomb', 'Juliette'

garden. Some are best in large-scale massed displays while others make good edging plants or potted plants. All are best grown in full sun but will tolerate almost any soil that does not become waterlogged. Regular removal of spent flower heads will greatly prolong the flowering season. All marigolds make good cut flowers but some people find their smell unpleasant in the house.
SEASON: African marigolds are best sown in spring. French marigolds can be sown in autumn in all regions but also in spring in cool areas. From sowing of seed to flowering takes about 12 weeks.

Marigold 'Boy-O-Boy Mixed'
This compact dwarf form grows only 20 cm high and so is ideal for edging and for low troughs or bowls. It is a French marigold with double crested flowers in a range of clear orange or yellow with some bicolours in deep red and orange. Space plants 15–20 cm apart.

Marigold 'Crackerjack'
An African-type marigold, 'Crackerjack' grows to 75 cm producing very large double flowers in shades of yellow and orange. This makes a striking display when mass planted, especially in large

gardens. Plants are sturdy but ideally
should have wind protection as they are
so tall. Space plants 30–40 cm apart.

Marigold 'Dwarf Double Mixed'
This is another French type with a dwarf
habit, growing to about 20 cm high. It is
often used to border garden beds and
lends itself to container growing. This is
ideal for those gardening on balconies,
especially where conditions are hot and
rather windy. Space plants 15–20 cm apart.

Marigold 'Honeycomb'
This is another popular double-flowered
form with deep red flowers being laced
and crested with rich gold. It is a small,
neat grower to 25 cm and produces a
profusion of blooms over a long season.
This French type should be spaced at
about 20 cm intervals.

Marigold 'Juliette'
This very striking variety has rich gold
and deep red flowers giving the effect of
flames. The red patterns on the petals
have great variety, making this a really
eye-catching flower for the garden or
pot. It is another French type, growing
only 30 cm high. Growth is compact and
flowering continues generally until well
into autumn. Space plants 20–25 cm apart.

MESEMBRYANTHEMUM 'LIVINGSTONE DAISY'
If you have a large sunny bank or rockery
to cover, this vividly coloured annual is
right for you. It can be grown very
effectively in hanging baskets too. It
tolerates poor soil as long as it drains well
and does well in exposed seaside gardens.
The daisy-like flowers come in shades of
red, pink, orange, cream, white and
mauve. All have a dark red eye and are
paler towards the centre. They bloom
from late winter through spring in warm
areas and during summer in cool regions.

Mesembryanthemum 'Livingstone Daisy'

They are prostrate growers, rarely
exceeding 8–10 cm in height. Space
plants 10–15 cm.
SEASON: Sow from late summer through
autumn in warm areas. In cool regions
sow in spring. Plants reach flowering
size in 4–5 months.

MIMULUS 'EXTRA CHOICE MIXED'
Mimulus or monkey flowers come in
dazzling colours that are patterned or
spotted to further increase their showy
appearance. Base colours are most often
in the red, yellow and orange range.

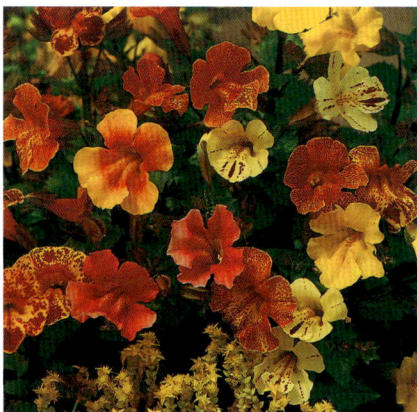
Mimulus 'Extra Choice Mixed'

Although strictly classed as perennial, these are best grown as annuals. In cool to mild areas they flower from middle to late spring through summer, in warm areas in spring only. Mimulus appreciates some shade and thrives in permanently moist soil. In cool climates, where it is most at home, it can be grown in more open, sunny positions but it prefers semi-shade. Plants grow 25 cm high and should be spaced 20–25 cm apart.
SEASON: Sow seed under cover in late winter or outdoors in spring to early summer. Plants will reach flowering size in 12–16 weeks.

NASTURTIUM

One of the most cheerful and easiest annuals to grow is the nasturtium. It has large seeds that are easy to handle and good results can almost always be guaranteed. These colourful flowers will grow in poor soil and will continue to thrive even in fairly dry conditions. They must be grown in full sun to flower well. The plants vary in habit from low, mounded bushes to long trailing types. Both flowers and leaves are edible. Flowering may be from mid-spring through summer, sometimes into autumn. Pinch out the growing tips occasionally to force branching and more flowers.
SEASON: Sow seed from early spring through to late summer. From seed to flower takes only 10 weeks.

Nasturtium 'Alaska'
This compact bushy plant grows 30 cm high and has green foliage striped and mottled in cream. Flowers are in strong bright colours of red, yellow and orange. Space plants about 25 cm apart.

Nasturtium 'Jewel Mixed'
This is one of the most popular selections with lovely semi-double flowers in colours of scarlet, yellow, cream and orange, many with contrasting colours in the throat. This is a small bushy grower to about 25 cm. Space plants about 25 cm apart.

Nasturtium 'Moonlight'
Flowers on this trailing or climbing nasturtium are an unusual shade of rich creamy yellow. This is a vigorous grower that can be used as a groundcover or planted to trail over walls or climb up fences. Plants will grow about 1.8 m and should be planted about 25 cm apart for good cover.

Nasturtium 'Peach Melba'
Compact growing to about 25 cm, this lovely variety has semi-double flowers in soft cream to pale yellow. Flowers are marked with orange-scarlet in their centres. This makes a lovely container plant but is also good for massed garden display, spaced at 20–25 cm intervals.

Nasturtium 'Salmon Baby'
One of the prettiest of all nasturtiums is this semi-double ruffled variety that is soft salmon to apricot in colour. The dark foliage is green to bronze, further highlighting the flowers. This forms a small, rounded bush about 25 cm high. Space plants 20–25 cm apart.

Nasturtium 'Tom Thumb'
Another bushy grower, 'Tom Thumb' has bright single flowers in shades of red, yellow, orange and salmon. Plants grow 25–30 cm high and should be spaced 25 cm apart.

Nasturtium 'Trailing Mixed Colours'
This vigorous grower will reach 1.8 m in a very short time in warm weather. It can be used to trail or climb, doing well even in poor soil. The single flowers are mainly in the orange, yellow and red range but most have pretty, contrasting markings. Plant 25–30 cm apart.

Top left to right: Nasturtium 'Alaska'; 'Jewel Mixed'; 'Moonlight'. Centre left to right: 'Peach Melba'; 'Salmon Baby'. Above left to right: 'Tom Thumb'; 'Trailing Mixed Colours'

NEMESIA

Although nemesia does not have as long a flowering period as some annuals, it is worth a place in the garden for its bright colours. It branches strongly from the base and makes a good filler to plant between bulbs to disguise the fading foliage. It should be planted in drifts for best effect but makes a good container plant too. Plants grow 25 cm high and should be planted 10–15 cm apart. Nemesia does best in full sun in well-drained soil that has been enriched with organic matter. It is not a good cut flower but if plants are cut back after the first blooming you may get a second crop of flowers. It flowers from late winter into spring in warm regions and in summer in cool areas.

SEASON: Sow seed in autumn to early winter, or in spring in cool areas. Plants take about 14 weeks from sowing of seed to flowering.

Nemesia 'Carnival Mixed'

This is a brightly coloured mix that includes red, yellow, cream, white, pink and blue flowers.

Nemesia 'Fire King'

Nemesia 'Fire King', which is less often seen, has vivid scarlet flowers that make a brilliant splash of colour in the garden. This variety is included in the Granny's Garden range.

NEMOPHILA 'BABY BLUE EYES'

Not as well known as it should be, this pretty plant has china blue flowers with a white eye. A small, neat grower to about 15 cm, this is ideal for edging garden beds, for growing in pockets in rock gardens or for container growing. It also makes a good companion for spring bulbs. After planting the bulbs, sow seed directly around the bulbs—the effect can be enchanting. Nemophila can be grown in full sun in cool districts but is best

Top: Nemesia 'Carnival Mixed'
Above: 'Fire King'

Nemophila 'Baby Blue Eyes'

grown in partial shade in other areas. It prefers humus-rich soils that retain some moisture and will not tolerate very dry conditions. It is quite frost hardy and prefers cooler climates. Thin out the seedlings so that plants are spaced about 10–15 cm apart.

SEASON: Sow in late autumn or early spring. From seed to flowering takes about 12 weeks. In cool climates successive sowings can be made through spring and summer.

NIGELLA

Best known as love-in-a-mist, this is easy to cultivate and rewarding to grow. The pretty floral display is succeeded by unusual inflated seed pods that are very popular in dried arrangements. Nigella has fine, feathery foliage and each flower is fringed and slightly veiled by it. Growing about 45 cm high, plants need protection from wind. Grow them in full sun to partial shade in any kind of well-drained soil, spacing the plants 25 cm apart. Regular removal of spent flowers or cutting for the vase prolongs flowering. This ranges from spring through summer depending on climate. Seed pods for use in dried arrangements should be picked after they have dried on the plant, bunched and hung upside down in a dry, airy place to complete the process. Plants tend to self-seed if pods are not removed when ripe.

SEASON: Sow seed in autumn or early spring. From seed to flowering takes about 14 weeks.

Nigella 'Miss Jekyll Blue'

This is the best known of these old-fashioned cottage garden flowers and comes in a true clear blue colour. This variety is included in the Granny's Garden range.

Nigella 'Persian Jewels Mixed'

This selection produces flowers in shades of both pale and deep blue, pink, rose and white.

NOLANA 'BLUE BIRD'

Growing only 15 cm high, this small, spreading annual makes an excellent groundcover and an unusual pot plant. In summer it bears bright blue to purple trumpet-shaped flowers which have a white throat and a yellow eye. The leaves are slightly succulent. This flower will open fully only in full sun and will grow in any reasonably good soil that drains well. It is sometimes known as Chilean bellflower although this name properly

Top: Nigella 'Miss Jekyll Blue'
Above: 'Persian Jewels Mixed'

Nolana 'Blue Bird'

belongs to *Lapageria rosea,* the Chilean floral emblem. The flowers are not suitable for cutting.
SEASON: Sow year round except for midwinter and midsummer. Plants will take 14 weeks from seed to flowering. Space seedlings 10–15 cm apart.

PANSY

Lovely whether grown in massed garden displays or in pots, pansies are all-time favourites. Although strictly classed as perennials, they are most often grown as annuals. Low growing, many have darker centres resembling little 'faces'. Many are lightly scented and although stems are short they are often cut and floated in shallow bowls indoors. They have a very long flowering period from late winter to early summer in warm districts and from spring through summer in cooler areas. Regular dead-heading is a must if you want to keep plants blooming. Pansies can be grown in full sun or semi-shade. They thrive in humus-rich soils that drain well.
SEASON: Sow in late summer through to early winter, and in spring in cool districts. From seed to flowering takes 16 weeks.

Pansy 'Blackjack'
Producing velvety black flowers with a yellow eye, 'Blackjack' is a dramatic flower that needs careful siting so its dark flowers don't appear to recede into the background. Growing 15 cm tall, plants should be spaced about 15 cm apart.

Pansy 'Clear Crystals Mixed'
Flower colours include blue, mauve, yellow, apricot, red and white, many with deeper tonings in the centre. Plants grow 15 cm high. Space them 15 cm apart.

Pansy 'Jolly Joker F2'
The startling combination of bright orange and deep purple makes this a real traffic stopper. Plants are compact growers 15–20 cm high and should be spaced about the same distance apart.

Pansy 'Rippling Waters'
This is another striking pansy with its deepest blue flowers boldly edged in cream. It lends itself to mass planting in garden beds or containers but it would team well with other pansies or 'Creamery' alyssum. Plants grow 20 cm high and should be spaced 15–20 cm apart.

Pansy 'Swiss Giants Mixed'
Flowers in this mix are much larger than those in most other selections. Flowers seem even larger as they grow on compact 15 cm plants. Colours include crimson, burgundy, yellow, white and blue, all with dark centres. Space plants about 15–20 cm apart for a full effect.

Pansy 'Universal Mixture F1'
This is described as a super pansy on account of its vigorous growth, brilliant colour range and perfect flower form. There are numerous plain colours with darker centres and several interesting bicolours. Neat compact plants grow 15 cm high. Space about 15–20 cm apart.

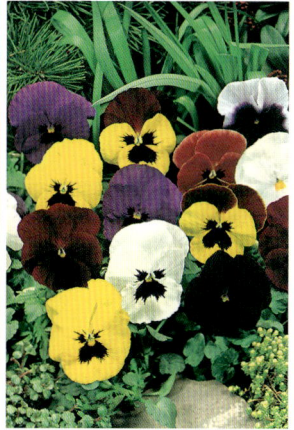

Top left to right: Pansy 'Blackjack'; 'Clear Crystals Mixed'; 'Jolly Joker F2'
Above left to right: 'Rippling Waters'; 'Swiss Giants Mixed'; 'Universal Mixture F1'

PENSTEMON 'MIXED COLOURS'

Although sometimes short-lived, this evergreen perennial gives great value in the garden, flowering from late spring through summer and sometimes into autumn. Cutting back the spent flower spikes encourages further blooming. Penstemon can be planted among shrubs or in massed garden displays with other perennials and annuals and is right at home in cottage gardens. Growing about 60 cm high, this selection includes some pretty varieties with tubular or funnel-shaped flowers in shades of pink, red,

Penstemon 'Mixed Colours'

purple, blue and white. Flowers mostly have a contrasting throat colour. It is best grown in full sun with wind protection in very well-drained soil. These plants tolerate light frost. Plants can be spaced about 20–30 cm apart.

SEASON: Sow seed in late summer and autumn, or spring in very cold regions. From seed to flower takes 5–6 months.

PETUNIA

Possibly the best of all the summer-flowering annuals for massed display, petunias also look wonderful in pots and hanging baskets. They thrive in hot, dry weather and perform poorly in wet summers. They need well-drained soil that has been enriched with organic matter. They flower from late spring through summer, sometimes into autumn if plants are cut back after the initial flowering. There is a huge colour range and they can be planted in mixed or single colours depending on the effect to be created. The seed is very fine and should be only just pressed into the surface of the mix.

SEASON: Sow seed in spring to early summer. From seed to flowering takes 12 weeks.

Petunia 'Confetti Mixed F2'

This selection will give you very free-flowering plants growing about 30 cm high. The single flowers will be pink, purple, white or red, creating a harmonious effect. Adaptable to any growing situation, plants should be spaced about 20 cm apart.

Petunia 'Resisto Mixed F1'

This compact grower represents a breakthrough in petunia culture as plants have been bred to recover quickly after rain. Seed is more expensive than for other selections but it is well worth it if your weather tends to be showery or overcast. The colours are vibrant red, purple, white, pink and cream, some starred with a contrasting colour. Growing about 25 cm high, plants should be spaced about 25 cm apart.

Petunia 'Supercascade Lilac F1'

Known as a grandiflora type, the fluted flowers of this variety may be 12 cm across. Branching from the base, plants grow about 30 cm high but can spread to 70 cm or more. Space plants 30 cm apart. This plant is ideal for hanging baskets and troughs.

Left to right: Petunia 'Confetti Mixed F2'; 'Resisto Mixed F1'; 'Supercascade Lilac F1'

PHLOX

Quick growing and long flowering, annual phlox makes an easy-care addition to the summer garden. Most varieties are small growers and make lovely massed displays of colour. With their compact growth they are ideal for containers or for edging garden beds. Flowers are flattish and carried in slightly rounded clusters. Some are lightly fragrant. They need full sun to flower well and prefer a rich soil that drains well. They are not generally used as a cut flower but small stems added to posies last fairly well. If plants are cut back after their first flowering they may bloom again. Most varieties should be spaced about 15 cm apart for a full display.

SEASON: Sow seed in spring through summer. From seed to flower takes about 10 weeks.

Phlox 'Brilliancy'

With neat, low growth this phlox forms a carpet of colour wherever it is planted. Plants generally grow 15–20 cm high and should be spaced 10–15 cm apart. Flowers come in various shades of pink, scarlet to crimson, mauve, purple, white and cream.

Top left to right: Phlox 'Brilliancy'; 'Cecily Old & New Shades'; 'Great Barrier Reef'
Above left to right: 'Tapestry'; 'Twinkle Stars'

Phlox 'Cecily Old & New Shades'

Many flowers in this range have a contrasting eye of colour in their centres. Space plants 15 cm apart. Plants grow about 20 cm high, producing flowers in rich cream and yellow, pink, salmon, blue and red: a really lovely selection.

Phlox 'Great Barrier Reef'

This selection has a very different colour range as it is a mix of salmon, apricot, pink, white and coral along with various shades of yellow. Growing 30–35 cm high, this selection brings the warmth of the tropics to your garden. Space plants 15–20 cm apart.

Phlox 'Tapestry'

By far the tallest of the phlox that are grown as annuals, these plants may reach 40–45 cm in height. Space plants 20 cm apart. Colours tend to be muted with many bicolours and some with picotee edges. The unusual colours include red, bronze, blue, mauve, purple, yellow and pink. This range gives a wonderful garden show and lasts well when cut.

Phlox 'Twinkle Stars'

With fringed or lobed flowers, these phlox are truly star-shaped. Flowers may be one solid colour—mainly red, pink or white—or two-toned in various shades of pink, cerise and white. This pretty variety grows about 20 cm high. Plants should be spaced 10–15 cm apart. Quite different from all other phlox, this selection makes an eye-catching show.

PINK 'OLD FASHIONED MIX'

See Dianthus (pages 56–7).

POACHED EGG PLANT

This cheery little annual (*Limnanthes douglasii*), is also known by the common name 'meadowfoam'. The slightly cupped flowers are bright yellow edged white

Poached egg plant

and grow on plants 15–25 cm high. It makes a lovely edging plant and is good for damp rockeries and for planting between pavers. It prefers full sun and a moisture-retentive soil. This is a versatile plant that does well in cool or warm regions. In warm climates the flowering display is through late winter to spring, in cool climates this is spring through summer. Space 10 cm apart for full cover. SEASON: Sow in autumn or spring for best results. From seed to flower takes about 16 weeks.

POLYANTHUS

In late winter or spring the bright cheerful flowers of polyanthus are guaranteed to lift the spirits. Whether planted in the ground in masses or just two or three in pots, the vibrant clear colours give an instant lift. Reliably perennial in cool climates, these are often cultivated as annuals, especially in warmer regions. They are best grown in partial shade in humus-rich soil. Protect plants from snails. Seed is very fine, so it can't be spaced for sowing. Plant established seedlings about 15 cm apart. SEASON: Sow in late summer to autumn. From seed to flower takes 18–24 weeks.

Polyanthus 'Gold Lace Polyanthus'

Included in the Granny's Garden range is this delightful old-fashioned type once widely grown for showing, especially in the north of England. There was fierce competition to see who could produce the most perfect plant. Mostly grown in containers, the flattish gold centred flowers are mahogany red with each petal outlined in gold. These perennials should flower for years as they can be increased by root division. Plants grow to about 20 cm high. These also like a humus-rich soil and partial shade.

Top: 'Polyanthus 'Gold Lace Polyanthus'
Above: 'Harlequin'

Polyanthus 'Harlequin'

Growing 20–25 cm high, the large flowers of polyanthus 'Harlequin' are clustered on stems that rise well above the bright green leaves. Flowers, most of which have a bright yellow eye, come in shades of rich blue, red, pink, yellow, white and cerise.

POPPY

Poppies are tall, showy annuals. All types should be grown in full sun, ideally with protection from strong wind. All need to be grown in well-drained soil that has been enriched with organic matter. Most make excellent cut flowers if they are picked as the buds are beginning to open. Scalding or burning the base of the stems will add greatly to the vase life of cut flowers. Poppies grow well in both cool and warm climates but are not suitable for the tropics. Seed can be sown in pots or trays but ideally should be sown where plants are to grow as they can be difficult to transplant. Depending on climate, plants will flower from late winter through spring or from late spring through to midsummer. Encourage blooming by carrying out regular dead-heading.

SEASON: Sow seed in late summer through to autumn. Plants will take from 16 to 18 weeks from seed until flowering.

Poppy 'Flemish Antique'

The large flamboyant flowers of poppy 'Flemish Antique' truly resemble those featured in Flemish and Dutch flower paintings of the seventeenth and eighteenth centuries. The peony-type flowers have a creamy background overlaid with varying shades of red, ranging from bright scarlet to deep burgundy. Plants will grow up to 90 cm high and should be spaced about 30 cm apart.

Poppy 'Iceland Mixed Colours'

Iceland poppies have open, silky flowers in shades of yellow, orange, red, pink and cream. Some Iceland poppies are bicolours. They give a great show in the garden if they are dead-headed regularly, but they are also truly wonderful for use as cut flowers. Plants grow about 40–60 cm high and should be spaced about 20 cm apart.

Poppy 'Shirley Double Mixed'

Shirley poppies tend to flower later than Iceland poppies even when grown in warm climates. They put on their best show in late spring. Most of the lovely double flowers in this range will be pink, red or white in colour. They will grow about 60 cm high and should be spaced about 20–30 cm apart.

Poppy 'Shirley Single Mixed'

Free-flowering and easy to cultivate, single Shirley poppies may be shades of red, pink or white with some being two-toned. This range also grows to about 60 cm and should be spaced about 20 or 30 cm apart. Shirley poppies have been derived from the European field poppy or Flanders poppy.

Top left to right: Poppy 'Flemish Antique'; 'Iceland Mixed Colours'
Above left to right: 'Shirley Double Mixed'; 'Shirley Single Mixed'

PORTULACA

These bright little succulents are also known as sun plants as their flowers usually open only in the sun. However, some of the newer hybrids remain open or partly so even when conditions are cloudy. Flowers are silky and come in almost every colour except blue. This is the perfect plant for hot, dry spots in the garden and for planting in pots and hanging baskets that dry out quickly. Portulaca grows well in any well-drained soil as long as it has maximum sun exposure. It is easy to grow and flowers through summer and often into autumn.

Top: Portulaca 'Double Mixed'
Above: 'Sundial Mixed F1'

SEASON: Sow in spring or early summer. From seed to flowering takes about 12 weeks.

Portulaca 'Double Mixed'

These ground-hugging plants grow 15–20 cm high and bear a profusion of fully double flowers in white, yellow, orange, scarlet, crimson, cerise and salmon. Plant 10–15 cm apart to ensure good cover.

Portulaca 'Sundial Mixed F1'

This mix grows about 20 cm high bearing double flowers that stay open longer in overcast conditions. Flower colours include salmon, white, various shades of pink and rose-red. This makes a particularly good container plant.

PRIMROSE 'SPRING PARADE'

Perennial in cool climates, this is often grown as an annual in warmer areas. Flowering is from late winter through spring. Mass plantings can create a kaleidoscope of colour, carpeting the ground. Plants grow only 15 cm high and the colourful flowers nestle down among the rosettes of slightly wrinkly leaves. Single plants can be grown in small pots

Primrose 'Spring Parade'

or several can be crowded into shallow bowls for a mini garden on a balcony. Plant about 10–15 cm apart in the garden but crowd them into containers. Protect them from snails that can ruin plants overnight. Grow in semi-shade or with morning sun only in humus-rich soil that retains some moisture.

SEASON: Sow seed in late summer to early autumn. From seed to flowering takes 18–24 weeks.

PRIMULA 'GILHAM'S WHITE'

Easy to grow, this annual primula has flowering stems that rise above neat clumps of bright green foliage. Popular for bedding or container growing, the chalk-white flowers appear in late winter or spring. Cut flowers last a few days in the vase. Although needing some shade in warm districts, primula can be grown in full sun in cooler climates. It must have humus-rich soil that holds some moisture but it does not tolerate waterlogging. Plants grow 20–30 cm high and should be spaced about 15 cm apart to provide a good show.

SEASON: Sow in late summer to autumn. Flowers will appear about 12–16 weeks after sowing.

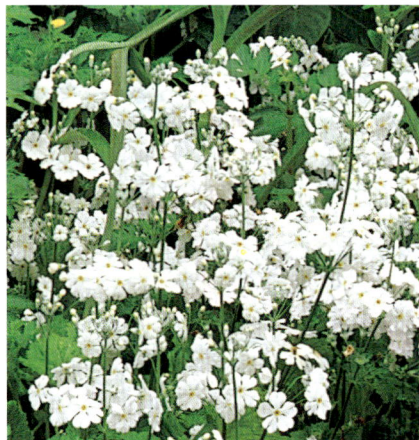

PRIMULA AND PRIMROSE

Primula and primrose seed should be left on or near the surface as this seed needs light in order to germinate strongly.

PYRETHRUM 'LARGE FLOWERED HYBRIDS'

This colourful perennial is very easy to grow and it makes a most colourful addition to mixed borders. It also makes an excellent cut flower. Cutting flowers for the house or regular removal of spent flowers will prolong the flowering display. Growing about 60 cm high, this plant produces its daisy-like flowers in summer. Flowers are a mixture of reds, pink and white with the stronger colours predominating. Grow in full sun in almost any kind of soil that drains well. Space plants 15 cm apart. This hardy herbaceous plant regrows year after year.

SEASON: Sow in autumn to early winter or in spring in cold climates. Plants will take about 12 weeks from sowing of seed to flowering.

Primula 'Gilham's White'

Pyrethrum 'Large Flowered Hybrids'

RUDBECKIA 'GLORIOSA DAISIES'

Known as coneflowers or marmalade daisies, these autumn-toned flowers bridge the gap between summer and autumn when many other flowers have finished. This is a tall grower to 90 cm and must be planted at the back of garden beds unless it is the centrepiece of a circular bed. Flowers are produced in abundance in shades of yellow, orange and mahogany. These give a long-lasting display but also cut well. They should be planted in full sun with some wind protection. Soil must drain well and, although rudbeckia is tolerant of poor soils, results will be much better if organic matter is dug in before planting. Ideally sow seed where plants are to grow, thinning to 40 cm between plants. SEASON: Sow in spring to early summer. Flowers will appear about 14 weeks after sowing.

Rudbeckia 'Gloriosa Daisies'

SALPIGLOSSIS 'BOLERO MIXED F2'

Rich colours are to be expected from this seed mix of showy annuals. Also called painted tongue, flowers are trumpet shaped with distinctive veins and patterning. Flower colours include red,

Salpiglossis 'Bolero Mixed F2'

crimson, pink, mahogany, yellow and purple. It makes a good cut flower but is probably better left for its spectacular garden display. Growing about 75 cm tall, it needs full sun and some wind protection although if close planted may be self-supporting. The floral display lasts from late spring through summer in warm areas. Seedlings are difficult to transplant and seed should be sown where it is to grow and later thinned to 15 cm spacings. Grow in well-drained humus-rich soil.
SEASON: Sow seed from early spring to early summer. Plants flower 12–14 weeks after sowing.

SALVIA

Also known as scarlet sage, salvia is one of the least demanding of all annuals. Today there are many varieties other than the plain red. All are easy to cultivate as long as they receive plenty of sun and are given free-draining soil. Widely used for mass displays in gardens, they do equally well in containers. Space plants 20–25 cm apart. They have a long flowering period through summer into autumn if the first flush of spent flowers is pruned off. In warm climates salvia that is cut back hard in autumn will sometimes grow and flower a second year.

SEASON: Sow in early spring in warm areas, late spring in cool zones. From seed to flowering takes about 16 weeks.

Salvia 'Blaze of Fire'

Growing to 30 cm, this fiery red annual flowers throughout summer. Team it with strong-coloured flowers such as marigold or celosia to create a 'hot' border.

Salvia 'Pharaoh Mixed'

With flowers of red, salmon-pink and purple streaked in white, this mix is a real novelty, providing something different for the summer garden. It grows 35 cm high and looks great in large troughs or tubs too.

SCHIZANTHUS

Butterfly orchid and poor man's orchid are two names commonly applied to this lovely plant. It creates a stunning show when mass planted in the garden or in pots and hanging baskets. It has pretty, fern-like foliage and produces a tapestry of brilliantly coloured flowers. Grown as a conservatory plant in cool areas, its main flowering is late spring to early

Top: Salvia 'Blaze of Fire'
Above: 'Pharaoh Mixed'

Top: Schizanthus 'Angel Wings Mixed'
Above: 'Gay Pansies'

summer. It can be grown in full sun or partial shade and must be given wind protection. It must have well-drained soil with added organic matter that helps to retain some moisture. Space plants 25–30 cm apart.

SEASON: Sow in late summer through autumn. From seed to flowering takes about 14 weeks.

Schizanthus 'Angel Wings Mixed'

Growing 30–35 cm tall, this selection produces brilliant trumpet-shaped flowers in rich tones of pink, purple and magenta, as well as soft creamy pastels and white. The flower centres are in a contrasting colour.

Schizanthus 'Gay Pansies'

This selection contains smooth pansy-shaped blooms in softer colours of pink, lavender and crimson, all with paler centres. Taller growing to 45 cm, it lends itself to garden bedding as well as being ideal for containers.

SNAPDRAGON

Colourful snapdragons are popular for garden display and as cut flowers. Children love to squeeze the backs of flowers to watch the mouth of the dragon open and 'snap' closed. They put on a long flowering display, which can be prolonged by cutting flowers for the house or dead-heading. Tall varieties must be grown towards the back of garden beds while dwarf forms make good edging plants and make a great show in pots and troughs. The colour range includes white, cream, yellow, orange, pink, red and lilac. Best grown in full sun, tall varieties must have wind protection. Soil must drain well, and plants benefit from mulching around their roots. In warm, humid seasons plants can be susceptible to the fungal disease rust. Tall growers should be

spaced 30–40 cm apart, dwarf forms 20 cm apart. You should sow the very fine seed by just pressing it into the surface of the mix.

SEASON: Sow seed from spring to autumn. From seed to flower takes 18–20 weeks.

Snapdragon 'Brighton Rock Mixed'

Included in the Granny's Garden range, this very striking old variety has flowers in a range of colours and is striped and blotched in contrasting shades of red, crimson and cerise. It grow 45 cm high and is sure to create enormous interest.

Top: Snapdragon 'Brighton Rock Mixed'
Above: 'Madame Butterfly F1'

Snapdragon 'Madame Butterfly F1'

This outstanding mix has a glorious range of open trumpet-shaped flowers quite unlike the traditional species. Growing vigorously, it may reach 75 cm; long stems can be taken when cutting for the vase. The full colour range is included.

Snapdragon 'Magic Carpet Mixed'

This mix produces neat, compact plants to 15 cm high in a full colour range. It is easier to grow and more reliable than taller strains and can be grown in containers, as edging to garden beds or to create a carpet of colour in the garden.

Top: Snapdragon 'Magic Carpet Mixed'
Above: 'Tom Thumb Mixed'

Snapdragon 'Tom Thumb Mixed'

Also covering the full colour range, this selection grows about 20 cm high.

STATICE

Although statice is possibly best known as a cut flower or in dried arrangements, it makes a bright addition to the summer garden, especially when mass planted. Although there are both annual and perennial types, most are grown as annuals. The actual flowers are small and white but it is the vibrantly coloured papery calyces that provide the colour. Purple is the most commonly seen colour but pink, yellow, apricot, white, blue and mauve can also be found. Plants flower over a long period through summer and a second flush can be encouraged by cutting back after the initial blooming. It must be grown in full sun but can be grown in any type of well-drained soil. It does best where summers are warm and dry and adapts well to exposed seaside gardens. Space plants 25–30 cm apart. To dry flowers cut them when in full colour, tie them in bunches and hang them upside down in a light, airy place.
SEASON: Sow in autumn or spring. Germination can be slow. Plants take about 20 weeks from seed to flower.

Statice 'Forever Formula Mixed'

Growing 45–50 cm high, this mix is part of the Flower Arrangers range. It contains the full bright colour range. It is lovely in the garden and cut flowers, used fresh or dried, retain their colour well.

Statice 'Special Mixed'

Also part of the Flower Arrangers range, plants in this selection grow as high as 60 cm. Both this and the shorter variety can be used to create a vibrant show in the garden when planted in generous swathes. You can continue to enjoy them through the seasons if you dry them.

Stock 'Ten Week'

Top: Statice 'Forever Formula Mixed'
Above: 'Special Mixed'

STOCK 'TEN WEEK'

The sweetly scented flowers of stock are always popular in garden displays and as cut flowers. Growing about 30 cm high, this range has sturdy, mainly double flowers in pink, white, cream, crimson, lavender and purple. This selection is not too tall to be grown well in containers also. Grow stock in full sun in humus rich, well-drained soil that has been limed before planting. Good drainage is essential as stock readily succumbs to root rot. Wind protection is desirable. Plant seedlings about 20 cm apart. This variety flowers over a long period from late spring through summer although the period will be shorter in warm areas. After cutting flowers, scald the stems. Stocks are subject to the same diseases as cabbages and related plants so don't plant them where any of these plants have been growing in the previous two years.
SEASON: Sow seed in late summer through autumn. Plants take from 5 to 6 months from seed to flowering.

STRAWFLOWER

Everlastings, paper daisies or strawflowers are names given to these bright flowers. They will reward you with a great show in the garden over many months to be followed by months or years as dried flowers indoors. The shiny, papery flowers come in a brilliant range of colours with many in pink, red, white, orange or yellow shades. Sometimes difficult to grow well in humid districts, they do best in areas with hot dry summers and cool winters. Plants tolerate light frost. They must be grown in full sun and look best when mass planted to create a meadow effect. Soil must be light and very well drained. There is a long flowering display through spring and

*Above left to right: Strawflower 'Dwarf Mixed';
'Tall Mixed'; 'Xeranthemum'
Below right: Helipterum 'Roseum Special Mixed'*

summer, sometimes extending into
autumn. Regular removal of spent flowers
helps to prolong flowering. For drying,
pick the flowers when the petals are well
formed but still curved in towards the
centre. Hang bunches upside down in a
dry, airy place. All of the strawflowers
described below are part of the Flower
Arrangers range.

SEASON: Sow in spring or autumn for
best results. From seed to flower takes
14–16 weeks.

Strawflower 'Dwarf Mixed'

The shortest of the strawflowers, this
selection grows about 45 cm high. Space
plants 15–20 cm apart. There is a good
colour range and plants tolerate harsh
growing conditions.

Strawflower 'Tall Mixed'

Growing up to 1 m high, these plants
need to be planted at the back of garden
beds or borders. Space them about
20–30 cm apart. Although this selection
has the full colour range it contains
stronger colours with many in red, burnt
orange or bronze tones.

Strawflower 'Xeranthemum'

This species of paper daisy has flowers in
various shades of pink, crimson and
white. It grows about 75 cm high and
with its softer tones can be easily blended
in with other pastel-coloured flowers.
You should space plants about
20–25 cm apart.

Helipterum 'Roseum Special Mixed'

Plants in this selection from Mr
Fothergill's Flower Arrangers range grow
35–45 cm high and flowers are in shades
of pink, red or white. This should be
grown in full sun in any type of fast-
draining soil with plants spaced
15–20 cm apart.

SUNFLOWER

Sunflowers delight both children and adults. They are easy to grow, seeds are large and easy to handle and the resulting flowers are large, bright and showy. Plants must be grown in full sun and must have wind protection as they grow so tall. Site them in front of a wall, fence or at the back of a garden bed. Quick growing, and tolerant of a wide range of conditions, growth is nevertheless improved by adding organic matter to the soil before planting. Plants are usually spaced about 30 cm apart. The bright yellow flowers light up the garden but they also make excellent cut flowers.

Top: Sunflower 'Dwarf Teddy Bear'
Above: 'Giant Single'

Scald stems after picking and use a heavy-based vase to prevent the top heavy flowers toppling it.

SEASON: Sow in spring to early summer. From seed to flower will take about 12 weeks.

Sunflower 'Dwarf Teddy Bear'

Although described as dwarf, and it is short compared with many sunflowers, this variety grows up to 90 cm high. The golden flowers are fully double and look quite fluffy at full bloom. Branching from the base, this produces more flowers per plant than other types.

Sunflower 'Giant Single'

Many gardeners, young and old, dream of growing the perfect giant sunflower. In some districts they even run competitions for them. Growing roughly from 2 to 4 m depending on conditions, they produce enormous bright yellow flowers that may be 25 cm across. Its rapid growth will be impressive too.

SWAN RIVER DAISY

With its fine ferny foliage and mounds of small daisies, this makes a lovely pot plant but it can also be grown in hanging baskets, in rockeries or as border plants or groundcovers. It has a long flowering period, mainly through summer and autumn, especially if it is shorn after the first flush of flowers has faded. In warm climates it will flower from spring onwards. It must be grown in full sun in very well-drained soil to look its best. If the aspect is too shaded it will grow long and lank and not flower well. To achieve good cover, plants should be spaced about 20 cm apart but much closer in containers.

SEASON: Sow in autumn or spring in warm areas, in spring to early summer in cool regions. From seed to flower takes about 16 weeks.

Left to right: Swan River daisy 'Brachycome–Blue Star', 'Brachycome–Bravo Mixed', 'Brachycome–Summer Skies'

Swan River daisy 'Brachycome–Blue Star'

Fine, feathery petals create these rich blue to purple star-like flowers. Plants grow about 30 cm high. The slightly cascading growth of this variety lends itself to growing in hanging baskets.

Swan River daisy 'Brachycome–Bravo Mixed'

Growth of this selection is compact, each plant forming a neat mound about 25 cm high. This lends itself to container growing but looks equally good as a garden edging. Colours include both pale and dark blue, violet, cerise and white, each flower having a contrasting eye.

Swan River daisy 'Brachycome–Summer Skies'

This is a mix of soft pastels, mainly mauve, pink and white. Flowers are lightly scented. Growing about 30 cm high, this lends itself to container growing but makes a lovely massed display in the garden too.

SWEET PEA

Everybody loves sweet peas for their fragrance and their lovely garden display.

Modern breeders have developed plants that bear larger flowers in greater numbers and plants suitable for tub culture as well as garden growing. They flower over a long season provided they are picked or dead-headed regularly. Sweet peas flower through late winter and spring in warm districts and through summer in cool areas. Best flowering comes from plants grown in full sun with protection from strong winds. The soil, which must drain well, should be prepared by digging in decayed manure or compost and lime before planting.

SWEET PEA SEEDS

Some sweet pea seed are small and look a little pinched, and some are round and plump. The small seeds are usually the dark colours such as purple, blue and shades of deep red or crimson, while the larger seeds are generally the white, cream and pale pink colours. Make sure that you sow all the seeds in the packet or at least some of each size.

Climbing types need the support of wire, lattice or bamboo stakes laced with string. Tall growers may reach 1.8 m while most dwarf types grow to 45 cm. Seed may be soaked overnight before sowing. Space plants 20–25 cm apart. Water thoroughly after planting and then restrict water until seeds germinate. SEASON: Sow from late summer through autumn in warm areas, spring in cool districts. From seed to flowering takes from 14 to 16 weeks.

Sweet pea 'America'
This lovely old variety has white flowers streaked in crimson. Flowers are somewhat smaller than many modern varieties but the perfume is glorious. This tall variety has good heat tolerance.

Sweet pea 'Bijou'
A good choice for small gardens or for trailing over walls and troughs, 'Bijou' mix contains flowers in blue, mauve, pink, red, white and maroon. Flowers are large and cut well. Bushes grow 45 cm high.

Sweet pea 'Cupani'
A tall, vigorous grower, 'Cupani' was introduced to Europe in 1699 by a Sicilian monk of the same name. It was probably the first sweet pea cultivated outside its native Mediterranean home. It is close to the original species with small, two-toned, heavily scented flowers in deep blue and burgundy.

Sweet pea 'Early Multiflora Gigantica'
This is a modern tall grower of great vigour with heavily perfumed flowers in a full colour range including pink, blue, mauve, scarlet and white.

Sweet pea 'Explorer Mixed'
A non-climbing variety, this sweet pea grows to 50–60 cm and so is ideal for trailing over walls and banks or for simply growing in containers or along the ground. Flowers have a good scent and the beautiful, clear colours range through shades of blue, pink, red and white.

Sweet pea 'Janet Scott'
Another fairly old variety, this was first introduced in 1903. Like many older types, flowers are smaller than modern varieties but heavily perfumed. This is a tall grower with good heat tolerance.

Sweet pea 'Lady Grisel Hamilton'
Described as shining silver lavender, this is certainly a delicately shaded flower. First introduced in 1899, it is tall, heavily perfumed and tolerates heat well.

Sweet pea 'Mammoth Mixed'
Early blooming and very free flowering, this modern selection grows tall and bears its sweetly fragrant flowers on long stems. This is a great variety to choose if cut flowers are your main concern.

Sweet pea 'Miss Willmott'
Named for the English gardener and writer of the same name, this was first introduced in 1901. Described as orange-pink with rosy overtones, this is another variety with smaller, heavily scented flowers with good heat tolerance.

Sweet pea 'Old Fashioned Old Spice Mixed'
Rich colour and heavy scent are features of this mix in the Granny's Garden selection. Tall growing, flowers are smaller than many modern varieties but are most prolific.

Sweet pea 'Painted Lady'
A lovely combination of white and pink flowers, this tall eighteenth century variety is small flowered but prolific in bloom. The strongly scented flowers are heat tolerant.

Top left to right: Sweet pea 'America'; 'Bijou'. Upper left to right: 'Cupani'; 'Early Multiflora Gigantica'; 'Explorer Mixed'. Lower left to right: 'Janet Scott'; 'Lady Grisel Hamilton; 'Mammoth Mixed'. Above left to right: 'Miss Willmott'; 'Old Fashioned Old Spice Mixed'; 'Painted Lady'

Sweet William 'Monarch Mixed'

Tagetes 'Lemon Gem'

SWEET WILLIAM 'MONARCH MIXED'

Related to carnations and pinks, sweet William provides colour in the garden through middle to late spring or summer, depending on climate. Growing about 45 cm high, it makes a delightful bedding plant. It is an excellent cut flower. Colours are in rich tones of pink, red, white, burgundy and bicolours. Although perennial, it is best grown as an annual in most climates. It should be grown in full sun in lightly limed soil that drains well. Space plants 20–30 cm apart in the garden but closer in containers.
SEASON: Sow from late summer through autumn or spring in cold districts. From seed to flowering takes 14–16 weeks.

TAGETES 'LEMON GEM'

Flowering from late spring through to early autumn, this dainty marigold grows only 15 cm high. It makes a pretty edging plant and is perfect for containers. The single, clear yellow flowers sit above fine, feathery foliage. To maintain flowering over the months regularly cut off spent blooms. Tagetes needs full sun for best results and moderately rich but well-drained soil. For dense cover, space plants 20 cm apart but wider spacings can be made as individual plants are capable of spreading 30–40 cm wide.
SEASON: In warm areas sow in autumn, elsewhere in spring to early summer. From seed until flowering takes 14–16 weeks.

THUNBERGIA 'BLACK-EYED SUSAN'

This slim-stemmed twining climber may grow from 1 to 2 m high. It is pretty grown in pots and hanging baskets but in the garden it could be grown up a

Thunbergia 'Black-Eyed Susan'

pyramid of stakes. It looks best where it can form a mound as growth can look sparse if spread thinly over a wide area. This plant is perennial in warm climates but is best grown as an annual. The flattish flowers may be orange, yellow or white, all with a very dark purple to black 'eye'. In warm regions it will flower from late spring through to autumn. Grow it in full sun in any type of well-drained soil. Sow several seeds per pot to create a full effect. This plant has escaped from gardens in some areas and has become a bushland weed. Take care not to let it escape if you live near bushland.

SEASON: Sow seed in early spring. Seed may be slow to germinate. Plants should flower in 14–16 weeks from sowing.

TORENIA 'CLOWN MIXED'

This bright variety of the annual wishbone flower will produce flowers in white, hot pink, purple or lavender, all with contrasting centres. It has a long flowering period from late spring or early summer right on into autumn if spent flowers are regularly removed. Growing only 20 cm high it will tolerate light shade but can be grown in full sun in cool areas. It prefers a well-drained soil

that has been enriched with organic matter to help retain some moisture. Space plants 20 cm apart in the ground, closer in containers.

SEASON: Sow seed from early spring through to early summer depending on climate. From seed to flower takes about 16 weeks.

VERBENA 'COMPACT MIXED'

Valued for its long flowering period, annual verbena can be used to create a carpet of colour in the garden. Growing only 15 cm high, it also makes a fine edging plant and a lovely plant for wide, shallow bowls and troughs. For denser groundcover it is suggested that lateral shoots be pegged down as they should then take root. Flowers in clustered heads are vibrant red, pink, purple and blue, most with a contrasting 'eye' of colour. Verbena will give you months of colour if spent flower heads are regularly removed. Best grown in full sun, it can be grown in any type of well-drained soil. Space plants 15–20 cm apart.

SEASON: It is best sown in autumn or spring but can be sown most times of the year except midwinter. From seed to flowering takes about 10 weeks.

Torenia 'Clown Mixed'

Verbena 'Compact Mixed'

Vinca 'Petite Mixed'

Viola 'Large Flowered Mixed'

VINCA 'PETITE MIXED'

Known by some as Madagascar periwinkle, this semi-succulent plant looks rather like impatiens or busy Lizzies. These plants flower for many months of the year, producing rose-pink, mauve or white flowers, some with a contrasting eye of colour. Plants are spreading and grow 20–30 cm high. Plants can be cut back after the first flowering and any time the growth gets open or untidy. Grow these massed in garden beds or in containers. Plant no more than 20 cm apart for a generous cover. Vinca can be grown in full sun or semi-shade. To carry plants through their long flowering, enrich the soil with compost or manure ahead of planting out. SEASON: Can be sown any time during the warm months or in autumn to early winter in mild districts. Flowering-size plants should take approximately 12 weeks from seed.

VIOLA 'LARGE FLOWERED MIXED'

This seed selection contains a lovely range of mainly clear coloured flowers although some have darker centres. Classed as a perennial, this plant is usually grown as an annual which will provide you with many months of colour if spent flowers are regularly removed. Colours range from white through yellow and apricot, to blue, mauve and rich reds. Growing about 15 cm high, plants should be spaced 15–20 cm apart. Although tolerant of partial shade, flowering will be

PLANTING UNDER TREES

Growing plants under trees is very difficult, as tree roots mat the ground and compete for both water and nutrients. Even if the soil is built up under a tree, which in itself could be harmful for the tree, the fine feeding roots of the tree will rapidly work their way into the new layer of soil. Lack of light may be a problem too, although you can let in more light by thinning the tree canopy. Only shade-loving plants that will tolerate both dryness and root competition thrive in these conditions. Vinca (periwinkle), ivy and clivias are among the few plants that grow well under trees.

better if the plant is grown in full sun. Enrich soil with organic matter before planting to maintain plants through their long flowering season.

SEASON: Sow seed from late summer to early winter or sow in spring in cool areas. Plants take about 16 weeks from seed to flowering.

VIRGINIAN STOCK 'FINEST MIXED'

The ideal filler plant, Virginian stock will often flower in six to eight weeks after sowing. It is good for edging garden beds and for growing in containers. Growing about 20 cm high, it is best sown where it is to grow and seedlings can be thinned to 6 or 8 cm spacings if necessary. Sow some seed every few weeks for a continuous display. The small, four-petalled flowers are lightly scented and come in shades of pink, lilac and white. Flowers are not suitable for cutting so plants should be pulled out once they are past their peak. Best grown in sun, this plant will tolerate shade for part of the day. Soil should drain well and acid soils should be limed before planting.

SEASON: Sow in late summer, autumn or early spring. From seed to flower takes 6–8 weeks.

VISCARIA 'BRILLIANT MIXED'

Catchfly or campion are names assigned to this pretty annual meadow flower. Best sown in large drifts, it should provide colour throughout late spring and summer. This mix contains flowers in pinks, reds, blues and whites. Flowers last surprisingly well when cut for the vase. Growing about 40 cm high, it is best sown where it is to grow and can be thinned later to 15–20 cm spacings. It should be grown in an open, sunny position in any type of well-drained soil.

SEASON: Sow in autumn to early winter or in spring. From seed to flowering takes about 12 weeks.

WALLFLOWER 'MONARCH FAIR LADY'

Wallflowers are loved for their velvety flowers that have a very distinctive sweet fragrance. They give a lovely show in the garden but also adapt well to container growing. In warm areas they flower in late winter to spring, in cool areas throughout spring. This fine selection contains flowers in colours of cream, yellow, rust and bronze, pink and purple. These make lovely cut flowers but water must be changed frequently for long vase

From left to right: Virginian stock 'Finest Mixed'; viscaria 'Brilliant Mixed'; wallflower 'Monarch Fair Lady'

life. The compact bushy plants grow about 30 cm high and should be spaced about 25 cm apart in the garden (closer in pots). Best flowering comes from plants grown in full sun but they will tolerate shade for part of the day. Soil must drain very well and lime should be added to acid soils before planting.
SEASON: Sow seed in late summer through autumn. From seed to flower takes 16–20 weeks.

ZINNIA

Zinnias are also known as youth and old age as new growth and flowering tends to obscure old fading flowers. Annual zinnias have a very upright growth habit. They look best in massed garden displays, and flowering will continue right through summer, sometimes into autumn. Zinnias make very good cut flowers if the stems are scalded after picking. There is a wide range of colours and growing heights. Tall varieties should be spaced 35–40 cm apart, smaller growers 25–30 cm apart. They must be grown in full sun and wind protection is necessary, especially for tall growers. Tolerant of almost any kind of well-drained soil, they will thrive in soils enriched with organic matter before planting. In very humid regions zinnias sometimes succumb to powdery mildew.
SEASON: Sow from spring to early summer. Zinnias take about 12 weeks from seed to flower.

Zinnia 'Carousel'
This is a really unusual mixture of muted bicoloured flowers. Growing 75 cm high, these are very different from the normal range of zinnias grown.

Zinnia 'Early Wonder Mixed'
This is a selection of really bright, showy flowers. Growing about 60 cm high, these can be sown where they are to grow to produce colour over a long season. Flowers range from cream and white, through yellow and burnt orange to various shades of pink, cerise and red.

Zinnia 'Haageana–Persian Carpet'
This compact, low-growing zinnia bears masses of double or semi-double flowers in mixed tones of gold, orange, mahogany and russet red. Flowers are weather resistant, not easily spoiled by rain. Growing 30–40 cm high, plants will spread to give good cover.

From left to right: Zinnia 'Carousel'; 'Early Wonder Mixed'; 'Haageana–Persian Carpet'

HERBS

Herbs are broadly defined by botanists as soft-wooded plants that may grow for a season or for several years. Humans have used herbs for thousands of years as flavourings in food, as medicines, as insect repellents, and in cosmetics and dyes. Herbs can be used fresh or dried and are generally easy to cultivate. Many will grow very successfully in containers as well as in the garden. There is nothing nicer than being able to pick some fresh herbs such as parsley, chives or rosemary to add to a meal you are preparing.

With few exceptions, their only requirement is a spot in full sun in reasonably well-drained soil. Many herbs have their origins in Mediterranean regions where they grow in often very poor stony ground. Herbs 'grown hard', that is without additional fertiliser and without lots of water, often have a better flavour than those grown in supposedly ideal conditions. Everyone with access to an outdoor area should be able to grow a pot or two of herbs. Herbs don't have to be grown in a separate herb garden; instead, they can be sown among flowering annuals, perennials or vegetables. Many are very decorative in themselves, and parsley is often used in bedding schemes to provide a ribbon of bright green. When planted in vegetable gardens some herbs can be helpful in warding off predatory insects, as their strong aromas mask the scent of the target plant, confusing the insects.

Purpose-built herb gardens, especially those in cool regions, often have paths and walls made of brick or stone which help store and reflect the heat that most herbs enjoy. In warm areas this is not necessary, although it is certainly an attractive look. In addition to a position in the warmest sunniest spot in the garden, well-drained soil is essential—you can open up heavier soils by digging in plenty of compost well before planting. If drainage is poor, try growing your herbs in raised beds in order to ensure success. It is best to avoid adding manure and fertiliser, but if you have an acid soil, lime should be dug in prior to planting. Dig in about 100 g of lime or dolomite per square metre or a little more if the soil has a high clay content. If growing in containers, add about a dessertspoon of lime to the potting mix in a 200 mm pot. More or less should be added according to container size. Most potting mixes formulated to a National Standard are suitable for herb growing, but for herbs such as sage it may be worth incorporating some coarse sand into the mix to achieve rapid drainage.

Many herbs are best sown directly where they are to grow. Most herbs grown as annuals will grow rapidly through the warmer months. Herbs such as basil are very cold sensitive, and if you live in a cool area you should not sow them until all danger of frost is over. Some will germinate very quickly in spring while others, including parsley, can be rather slow to appear. Allow plants to develop strongly before starting to harvest leaves, but once they are well established pick them regularly to ensure vigorous growth throughout the season.

BASIL

Basil is very much a warm season herb. It has a very distinctive aroma and is delicious added to salads, pasta and soups. Basil has a particular affinity with tomatoes. It is the main ingredient in pesto, a sauce of Mediterranean origin eaten with pasta. Although best used fresh, it can be dried by spreading bunches of leaves on wire trays and drying them in a cool, airy place out of the sun. It appreciates added organic matter in the soil or potting mix. It should be grown in full sun and growth will be rapid in warm weather. There are several different types of basil, the most popular being sweet basil. However, purple basil is decorative as well as tasty

SCENT

All herbs are pleasantly scented and will attract bees and butterflies, so put some in pots near the house as well as having them in their own part of the garden.

A SAMPLE HERB GARDEN

SPRING THROUGH SUMMER

Dill

Oregano

Mint

Thyme

Basil

Rosemary

Chives

Parsley

AUTUMN THROUGH WINTER

Sage

Oregano

Mint

Thyme

Rosemary

Lemon balm

Parsley

and lemon basil has a strong lemon
fragrance. Thai basil is also used as a
culinary herb. Growing heights will vary
with plant type but sweet basil will grow
30–45 cm high. Once growth is vigorous,
pinch out the growing tips to force
branching and make plants bushy. When
flower buds appear pinch them, out as
leaf growth will cease if they are allowed
to mature.
SEASON: Sow in spring and thin seedlings
to 30 cm apart. Pick leaves as needed
once plants are well developed.

Basil 'Gourmet Mixed'
Packed under the Gardening Australia
label, this is a mix of four types of basil,
'Sweet Genovese', lemon basil, purple
basil and Thai basil. All are easy to grow.

Basil 'Sweet Genovese'
As this is the most popular basil it is
packed separately. Many people want to
grow this basil in quite large quantities
for making pesto. It is both quick and
easy to grow.

BORAGE
The young leaves of borage add a
cucumber flavour to salads and cool
drinks. The pretty blue flowers are also
edible and often used to garnish food.
Annual borage is a vigorous grower and
mature plants tend to self-seed through
the garden. The whole plant is covered
with fine hairs and may grow to almost
1 m high. Flowers are nectar rich and
very attractive to bees, providing a source
for a delicious honey. Leaves can be used
fresh or frozen for later use but do not
dry well. Use only the young leaves as
older ones may be tough and coarse.
Flowers can be put into ice cube trays,
covered with water and frozen ready to
add later to cool drinks. Borage can be
grown year round in mild climates. It can
be grown in containers but is probably
better in the garden on account of its
size. This herb will grow in any type of
soil as long as it drains well.
SEASON: Best sown in spring or autumn
with plants spaced about 30 cm apart.

Top: Basil 'Gourmet Mixed'
Above: 'Sweet Genovese'

Borage

CHERVIL

Chervil is one of the annual herbs that make up the classic 'fines herbes' along with chives, tarragon and parsley. It has a delicate flavour and should always be used fresh. It is used in egg dishes and sauces, salads, soups and chicken dishes. Leaves are used fresh or they can be dried by spreading the leaves on a wire rack in a dry, airy place out of the sun. Plants grow about 30 cm high and have fine, fern-like leaves. Flat heads of white flowers appear in summer and they can be cut off if you don't want the plants to self-seed. This pretty looking plant is well suited to container growing. It will grow in any well-drained soil in sun or partial shade, and in warm areas should be given some shade in midsummer.

SEASON: Sow in spring through to autumn, thinning to 30 cm spacings.

Chervil

CHIVES

Chives are perennials, growing from a small bulb. Equally at home in pots or in the garden, they are used in dishes or as a tasty garnish. Harvest the leaves by cutting or by pinching out close to the ground. Easy to grow and very productive in warm weather, they can also be quite decorative when their flowers appear in late spring. However, it is wise to leave only a few flowers as flowering tends to exhaust the plants. In winter plants will die back to the bulb to reappear the following spring once the weather warms. Chives can be grown in sun or partial shade and need plenty of water during the growing season to promote growth and succulent stems. Any well-drained soil will suit. Chives grow from 20 to 30 cm tall and should be spaced 10–15 cm apart.

SEASON: Sow seed in spring through to early autumn. The first leaves should be ready for harvest in about 12 weeks.

Chives, regular

Chopped chives will give a mild onion flavour to food. They have pink to mauve coloured flowers.

Top: Regular chives
Above: Garlic chives

Garlic chives

The mild garlic flavour of these chives adds a subtle flavour to salads, soups, vegetables and stir fries. Unlike regular chives these have a broader, flat leaf and flowers are white.

CORIANDER

There are different strains of coriander that are grown either for their leaves or seeds. This annual variety will grow very rapidly in warm weather, flower and produce large quantities of spicy seed. The crushed seeds are an essential ingredient in curries but are also used to flavour meat, fish and poultry. They are also used to add an interesting zest to cakes and biscuits and may be sprinkled over fruit being baked. Coriander has strongly aromatic, feathery leaves and plants grow 45–60 cm high. Flowers are white and frothy. Seed is harvested when the heads turn a light brown. Dry the

SOWING CORIANDER

Coriander matures quickly and can be fairly short lived in the garden. Therefore, make successive sowings for a continuous supply.

seed heads and shake out the seeds for storage in airtight containers. Plants should be grown in full sun with protection from strong wind. Coriander needs well-drained soil with a little added organic matter.

SEASON: Sow seed in spring through to autumn, spacing the plants about 20 cm apart.

DILL

Dill is the classic flavouring for fish dishes but is also a fine accompaniment to salads, vegetables, rice and egg dishes. Dill seeds are used in pickling but are also added to coleslaw and cabbage dishes, various breads and pastries. Dill is used fresh or dried and can also be frozen. Dry the fine, hair-like leaves on wire racks in a cool, airy place. Dill bears its flattish heads of yellow flowers in summer. As flowers die off, seed sets. Seed heads are gathered in autumn when they have turned brown. They can be spread on trays and dried in the sun for a few days. Dill is a tall-growing annual that may reach 90 cm in height. It should be grown in full sun with wind protection, and grows in any kind of well-drained soil.

SEASON: Sow seed in spring to early autumn. Space plants 25 cm apart.

Coriander

Dill

LEMON BALM

The foliage of this soft-leaved herb has a strong lemon fragrance. Leaves can be used to make a refreshing tea or added to fruit drinks. They are sometimes used as a lemon substitute and can be added as seasoning to fish and chicken dishes as well as to fresh or stewed fruit. To dry leaves spread them on racks in a cool, airy place or wrap sprigs in foil and freeze them for later use. Lemon balm is easily grown in sun or partial shade and makes a good ornamental groundcover. It can be vigorous in warm climates, spreading by underground runners. It does best in soils that do not dry out too rapidly in summer. Plants grow 30–45 cm high and should be spaced about the same distance apart. This perennial plant does not tolerate frost and so may need to be grown as an annual in cool regions.
SEASON: Sow from spring to early autumn. In cool areas sow in spring only.

Marjoram

Lemon balm

MARJORAM

Sweet marjoram is perennial in warm climates but is grown as an annual in cooler areas. It is a compact plant that will grow from 45 to 60 cm high. In the garden, space plants about 20 cm apart. A versatile herb, it is used in meat and poultry dishes, with vegetables (especially tomatoes) and in soups and sauces. Marjoram has a long history of culinary and medicinal use and was traditionally considered the symbol of happiness, youth and beauty. It should be grown in full sun in well-drained soil but should be given regular watering in dry weather. Plants can be cut back each year at the end of winter to promote fresh growth. Sprays of leaves can be hung in bunches in a dry, airy place until they can be stripped off the stem and stored in airtight containers.
SEASON: Seed can be sown year round except in midsummer and midwinter.

MINT

Mint is one of the few herbs to do well in shade and damp soil. It can be very invasive and so may need to be confined with some sort of root barrier in the garden or grown in a container. Mint is the classic accompaniment for lamb and green peas but also adds flavour to new potatoes, tomatoes and some shellfish. It makes a refreshing addition to cool summer drinks. Mint is a perennial that can be regrown from the smallest root once it is established. With plenty of moisture, mint grows quickly through the warmer months and should be cut back hard in late winter to ensure a crop of

Mint

Oregano

fresh new leaves. Plants can grow to about 45 cm high but with regular picking of leaves it is unlikely to grow taller. Space seedlings about 20 cm apart. Mint sprigs can be wrapped in foil or chopped finely and put into ice cube trays with a little water and then frozen for later use. Leaves can also be hung in bunches for drying in an airy place and then stored in airtight containers.

SEASON: Seed can be sown year round but it is best to avoid winter as germination will be very slow.

OREGANO

Oregano has a strong pungent aroma and flavour that is the perfect addition to many dishes of Mediterranean origin. It is added to pizza and pasta, lamb and other meats, and many sauces and vegetables. This perennial will grow year round in warm climates but is grown as an annual in cool areas. Even in warm gardens plants need replacing every three to four years. In warm gardens it can be grown as an edging plant or as a spreading groundcover. It must be grown in full sun in very well-drained soil and is easy to cultivate in containers. Plants grow 30–45 cm high and should be spaced 15–20 cm apart. Oregano is a wild form of marjoram to which it is closely related.

The flavour is similar but oregano has a much more robust flavour.

SEASON: Seed can be sown in spring or autumn.

PARSLEY

Parsley is probably the best known of all the herbs. Although truly a biennial it is most often grown as an annual. It is used in a wide variety of both cold and hot dishes and is popular as a garnish. Parsley is rich in iron and vitamin C and should be eaten fresh as much as possible. Parsley can also be dried or frozen for later use. It can be grown in the garden or in pots. Parsley is often grown in the flower garden to provide a strong, rich green colour. It is not difficult to grow but seedlings may be slow to germinate, generally taking 3–4 weeks to emerge. Grow parsley in sun or partial shade in rich soil and give it plenty of water. Keep this plant growing strongly by giving it occasional liquid fertiliser or use a slow release fertiliser. Plants grow about 25 cm high and should be spaced 20–30 cm apart in the garden but 2–3 can be crowded into a 200 mm pot.

SEASON: Sow seed from spring through to early autumn. Start picking small sprigs for use in cooking once the plants are growing strongly.

Left to right: Parsley 'Curlina'; 'Italian Plain Leaved'; 'Moss Curled'

Parsley 'Curlina'

Sold in the Vegetables range, this is a compact, densely curled variety that will produce an abundance of rich green leaves. Once it is growing strongly it can be picked frequently as it will continue to push out more growth.

Parsley 'Italian Plain Leaved'

With a stronger flavour than the curled varieties, this parsley is popular in Mediterranean cooking. The leaves are flat but attractively dissected. It gives a more robust flavour to sauces.

Parsley 'Moss Curled'

This very curly-leaved parsley is a vigorous grower as long as it is given fertile soil and ample watering. Plants generally grow from 20 to 30 cm high.

ROSEMARY

Rosemary is a perennial woody shrub growing about 1 m high and round. It is traditionally used with lamb but is an important ingredient in many dishes of Mediterranean origin. It is used with fish, soups and stews and in a number of vegetable dishes. Rosemary is the symbol of remembrance, love and fidelity. In ancient times this herb was thought to strengthen the memory and so garlands of rosemary were worn by Greek scholars when sitting for exams. Rosemary should be grown in an open, sunny position in very well-drained soil. Space seedlings 30–40 cm apart to allow for spread. Grow it where it is brushed in passing so that its lovely aroma can be enjoyed. Plants benefit from an occasional overall pruning as this helps keep bushes compact and ensures plenty of young, fresh growth. It can even be grown as a

Rosemary

hedge. Rosemary leaves can be used fresh or dried. For drying, cut stems before plants flower and hang bunches in a dry, airy place until they strip easily from the stalks. Sprigs of rosemary can also be wrapped in foil and frozen for later use. SEASON: Sow seed from spring to autumn. Do not sow too early in spring as seed will not germinate in cool conditions.

SAGE

Sage is traditionally used to counteract the richness of some meats and poultry. It is used in stuffings but is also popular for use in soups, sauces, vegetable and egg dishes. Sage is an aromatic perennial that will grow about 60 cm high. Plants should be spaced about 30 cm apart in the garden. It has a long history of use as a medicinal herb. Sage is not hard to grow as long as it is grown in perfectly drained soil in full sun. It will grow well even in quite dry conditions once it is established and it is easily grown in containers. This herb should never be overwatered as it will quickly die of root rot. Sage leaves can be used fresh or dried. Bunches of leaves can be hung upside down in a dry, airy place or spread on racks to dry.
SEASON: Sow seed from spring through to autumn.

THYME

Garden thyme is a perennial herb that can be easily blended into the ornamental garden as a groundcover or carpeting plant. Growing to only about 20 cm in height, and often less, thyme can be grown in the garden in pockets between paving stones or used as an edging plant. It should be spaced at intervals of about 20–30 cm. Thyme also does well in pots and other containers. It must be grown in full sun in soil that drains freely. As a culinary herb it has a great number of uses; for example, it is one of the ingredients of the traditional bouquet garni together with parsley, marjoram and bay leaf. It is also used as a flavouring in poultry dishes, meat dishes, vegetables, soups and stews and is often used in herb bread. Thyme is easy to grow and is very pretty in flower, when it will be extremely attractive to bees—thyme honey is very popular in Mediterranean countries. You can harvest the leaves as you need them and use them fresh in cooking, or you can hang sprays of leaves in bunches for drying and storing. Sprigs of thyme leaves securely wrapped in foil are suitable for freezing for later use.
SEASON: You should sow seed from spring through to autumn.

Sage

Thyme

VEGETABLES

There is nothing to equal the flavour of vegetables picked fresh from your own garden. Many commercially grown vegetables are selected for their uniform appearance, ease of transport and long shelf life, at the expense of truly satisfying flavour. Your home-grown produce will be packed full of vitamins as it goes straight from the garden into salads or the saucepan. Growing your own vegetables from seed allows you to select from a great range of the best varieties, both old and new. You can sow small amounts of seed in succession throughout the season according to your particular household needs, which will ensure a long harvesting period.

Today's vegetable garden contains plants originating in many different parts of the world, most far removed from their original species due both to natural selection and breeding. Vegetables have been cultivated for millennia. China and other parts of Asia have a long history of vegetable cultivation, and archaeologists have uncovered seeds of plants grown by the ancient Egyptians, Romans and Greeks similar to those grown today. In Mexico and South America, maize (corn), beans and squash have been cultivated for thousands of years. Throughout the centuries, we have been dependent on cultivated vegetables for food.

Select a site for your vegetable garden where it will receive sun for a minimum of six hours a day. The size of your vegetable garden will depend not only on the available space but also, more importantly, on how much time you have to care for it. Even in small spaces you can grow vegetables you enjoy eating and crops that do not require much space. For example, carrots, radish and shallots take up little space, and climbing peas and beans take up little room at ground level. Vegetable gardens require more attention than the flower garden as vegetables must be grown quickly to ensure the best-quality produce. You should carry out very regular watering, weeding, feeding and checking for pests. Vegetables can of course be grown in the flower garden, but it is easier to look after them in a dedicated space. Soil must be well prepared and drainage must be good. If drainage is not good, raise the beds or grow your vegetables in containers. Use lots of organic matter to improve soil structure, to supply and retain nutrients and to either hold water in light soils or open up heavier soils. If growing vegetables in containers, use a quality potting mix and if necessary add extra compost or decayed manure. Both containers and garden beds should be mulched with organic matter.

Crop rotation

To lessen pest and disease problems, ideally you should not grow the same crop or crop from the same family in the same patch of garden each year. Different crops use nutrients in different ways, too, so that soil can be depleted of these nutrients despite your best preparation. The lists below will help you identify the groups to which your vegetables belong. To make crop rotation easier, keep records of what you plant and where.
• Cabbage, Chinese cabbage, cauliflower, broccoli, Brussels sprouts, kohlrabi, radish, swede, turnip, mustard greens
• Tomato, capsicum, pepper or chillies, eggplant, potato
• Pea, broad bean, dwarf bean, climbing bean
• Pumpkin, squash, melon, cucumber, zucchini, marrow
• Carrot, parsnip, celery, parsley
• Silver beet, beetroot, spinach
• Lettuce, globe and Jerusalem artichoke
• Onion, garlic shallot, leek, chive

In the home garden crops may need to be grown in the same area more frequently than they should be, but try to rotate crops as the reduction in disease (especially soil-borne disease) is considerable. Grow your vegetables according to the appropriate season. If you try to grow them out of season the results will be very poor.

FILLING ODD SPACES

Lettuce, radish, spring onion, beetroot and carrot are quick and easy to grow—and can be sneaked into odd spaces in the flower garden.

A SAMPLE VEGETABLE GARDEN

SPRING THROUGH SUMMER

Cucumber
Climbing bean
Silver beet
Capsicum
Dwarf bean
Turnip
Shallot
Parsnip
Tomato
Oregano
Rosemary
Parsley
Iceberg lettuce   Carrot   Beetroot   Spring onion   Radish

AUTUMN THROUGH WINTER

Telephone pea
Snow pea
Turnip
Broccoli
Cabbage
Cauliflower
English spinach
Oak-leaf lettuce
Parsnip
Rocket
Oregano
Rosemary
Parsley
Iceberg lettuce   Carrot   Beetroot   Onion   Radish

HARVESTING VEGETABLES FROM THE HOME GARDEN

SPRING

Artichoke	Chinese cabbage	Lettuce	Silver beet
Beetroot	Chinese mustard	Mustard	Spinach
Broad bean	Cress	Pak choi	Spring onion
Cabbage	Endive	Pea	Swede
Carrot	Kohlrabi	Rocket	Turnip

SUMMER

Artichoke	Chinese mustard	Marrow	Rocket
Bean	Chopsuey greens	Melon	Shallot
Beetroot	Cress	Mustard	Silver beet
Cabbage	Cucumber	Okra	Spring onion
Capsicum	Eggplant	Onion	Squash
Carrot	Endive	Pak choi	Sweet corn
Celery	Kale	Parsnip	Tomato
Chicory	Lamb's lettuce	Pumpkin	Zucchini
Chinese cabbage	Lettuce	Radicchio	

AUTUMN

Bean	Chinese cabbage	Marrow	Rocket
Beetroot	Chinese mustard	Melon	Salsify
Broccoli	Cress	Mustard	Shallot
Cabbage	Cucumber	Okra	Silver beet
Capsicum	Eggplant	Onion	Spring onion
Carrot	Endive	Pak choi	Squash
Cauliflower	Lamb's lettuce	Parsnip	Sweet corn
Celery	Leek	Pumpkin	Tomato
Chicory	Lettuce	Radicchio	Zucchini

WINTER

Broccoli	Chinese mustard	Lettuce	Rocket
Cabbage	Chopsuey greens	Mustard	Salsify
Carrot	Cress	Okra	Spinach
Cauliflower	Kale	Pak choi	Spring onion
Chicory	Kohlrabi	Parsnip	Swede
Chinese cabbage	Leek	Pea	Turnip

ARTICHOKE 'GREEN GLOBE'

Globe artichokes are a gourmet delight. The plants they grow on are very attractive with large, silvery divided leaves that provide a strong decorative accent. Plants grow about 1.5 m high and should be spaced almost 1 m apart. Good soil preparation is essential for good quality crops—grow artichoke in a well-drained soil heavily enriched with organic matter. The above-ground parts of the plant die back to the base each year and regrowth starts from the roots the following spring. The edible part of the artichoke is the solid centre of the flower bud and the fleshy bracts at the base of it. The buds should be picked before the scales open out.

SEASON: Sow seed in early spring to early summer. From seed to harvest takes about 40 weeks. In warm frost-free areas sow in autumn too.

Artichoke 'Green Globe'

BEAN

Beans are warm-season vegetables that with regular picking will crop over a long period. Once cropping has begun, pods should be picked every 4–5 days. Generally, climbing beans crop more heavily than dwarf beans and can be harvested over a longer period. Sow into moist, well-prepared soil when all danger of frost is over and the soil has started to warm. After sowing, water the seed in lightly and do not water again until seedlings appear or the seed will rot in the ground. Support for climbing beans should be in place before sowing. Spraying flowers gently with water helps pod set. In warm, humid conditions beans can be prone to rust, a fungal disease.

SEASON: Sow seed in spring through summer. From seed to cropping takes 8–12 weeks. Space seeds 10–15 cm apart.

Bean, dwarf bean 'Banjo'

'Banjo' is a high-yielding stringless bean with very smooth uniform pods. It has good disease tolerance and performs well under a wide variety of conditions.

Bean, dwarf bean 'Purple Queen'

The glossy purple pods of this variety turn green when cooked. It has excellent flavour and is almost stringless when harvested young. It produces high yields.

Bean, dwarf bean 'Snap Bean'

Pods of this bean are quite small but have a good flavour. It is stringless and crops well. Pods are mostly cooked whole.

Bean, climbing 'Blue Lake'

One of the most delicious varieties, 'Blue Lake' produces heavy crops of rounded stringless beans. It grows to 2 m and needs poles or trellis for support. It does well in areas with cooler summers.

Bean, climbing 'Epicure'

Another tried and true favourite, 'Epicure' has an excellent flavour. It is almost stringless and crops reliably.

Bean, climbing 'Purple King'

Children love to see the purple pods turn green during cooking. Pods are fairly flat and are stringed, but not heavily. It yields very well.

Top left to right: Dwarf bean 'Banjo', dwarf bean 'Purple Queen'. Centre left to right: Dwarf bean 'Snap Bean', climbing bean 'Blue Lake', climbing bean 'Epicure'. Above left to right: Climbing bean 'Purple King', climbing bean 'Scarlet Runner', climbing bean 'Snake Bean'

Bean, climbing 'Scarlet Runner'

This succulent bean has flat, slightly rough pods and very ornamental scarlet flowers. It is a perennial that dies back after cropping to regrow the following spring. It will crop successfully only in areas with relatively cool summers. In warm areas it will flower but not set pods.

Bean, climbing 'Snake Bean'

This bean is suited to very warm or tropical districts. The narrow stringless pods grow to 30 cm long. Pick when young for best flavour and texture.

BROAD BEAN

Broad beans grow through the cool season and are ready for harvest in spring to early summer. Harvest pods when young or allow to grow on until the seeds have reached a good size. Acid soils should be limed and well enriched with organic matter before seed is sown. Plants can grow 1.5 m high, becoming quite bushy. They are often sown in double rows 30 cm apart. If more than one double row is to be sown allow 60–75 cm between the double rows. Plants may flower early but pods will not set until the days warm and lengthen in spring. Once a good crop of pods has set, pinch out growing tips to encourage development of the pods. Aphids may become a problem in spring and should be controlled.

SEASON: Sow from autumn into winter. From seed to maturity takes 18–20 weeks.

Broad bean 'Coles Early Dwarf'

Growing from 1–1.5 m high, this is not a very dwarf plant. It is a strong grower with some wind resistance that produces flavoursome medium-sized pods.

Broad bean 'Early Long Pod'

This bean grows to 2 m high. Pods may grow 20–25 cm long. A 5–6 m row of plants is enough for the average family.

WHEN TO SOW BROAD BEANS

Sow late in autumn rather than early. Late-sown plants grow quickly in the warmth of spring and will catch up with earlier sowings. Later sowings flower as the weather warms up, avoiding flower drop and producing better crops. Warm weather is needed for a good crop.

Left to right: Broad bean 'Coles Early Dwarf'; 'Early Long Pod'

BEETROOT

Beetroot is eaten fresh, pickled or as a
hot vegetable. Beetroot tops are tasty and
nutritious if harvested when young.
Today's range of beetroots vary greatly in
shape and size. Seed is best sown where
it is to grow and spaced according to the
variety grown. Average size beets are
spaced 10 cm apart while baby beets
need only 5 cm spacings. Beetroot must
be grown quickly and regular fertilising
and watering are essential. As they grow
the roots will push up above the soil.
This is natural: don't cover with soil. Pull
or dig the roots when they reach the size

you prefer. Beetroot needs well-prepared,
lightly limed humus-rich soil.
SEASON: Sow seed in late winter or early
spring through to autumn. From seed to
harvest takes from 10 to 15 weeks.

Beetroot 'Boltardy'

This is a particularly fine variety as it
resists bolting (going to seed) in hot
weather. The beets are spherical and very
uniform with a good flavour and colour.

Beetroot 'Crimson Globe'

This fine-flavoured variety is globe
shaped. It is a rich red and lends itself to
any type of preparation.

Beetroot 'Detroit 2–Nero'

Although these beets will in time reach a
diameter of around 8 cm this variety, part
of the Little Wonders range, is usually
grown to be harvested when no more
than the size of a ping-pong ball. These
dark red baby beets are sweet and ideal
for serving whole in salads.

Beetroot 'Forono'

Easy to slice, 'Forono' is a long cylindrical
beetroot that is slow to turn woody. It
has a good flavour and texture, and its
uniform slices present a good appearance
on the plate.

Top left: Beetroot 'Boltardy'. Above left to right: 'Crimson Globe'; 'Detroit 2–Nero'; 'Forono'

Left to right: Broccoli 'Emperor F1', 'Italian Sprouting', 'Jewel F1'

BROCCOLI

Broccoli is a cool-season vegetable grown for its densely packed heads of flower buds. It is highly nutritious and a great source of dietary fibre. After the main heads are cut, side shoots appear that will form smaller but no less tasty heads. Heads should be harvested when they are full and rounded but before any of the flowers turn yellow. For best results soils should be enriched with organic matter and dressed with lime before planting. Plants can become top heavy as they grow so the soil should be hilled around the base to make them more stable. They can also become quite wide and should be spaced 60 cm apart. Broccoli is susceptible to cabbage moth and cabbage white butterfly; look out for caterpillars. SEASON: Seed is sown in late summer to autumn. From seed to first harvest takes from 16–20 weeks.

Broccoli 'Emperor FI'

This is a robust grower producing heavy heads early in the season. It can be sown in late summer for cropping in autumn.

Broccoli 'Italian Sprouting'

With a medium-sized central head and numerous side shoots, this variety crops over a long period. Previously this type of broccoli was the main variety grown.

Broccoli 'Jewel FI'

The fine variety from the Little Wonders range produces mini heads of broccoli that can be served as individual portions. It can also be grown on for heads to mature into a larger size but it is valued for its good crop of small compact heads early in the season.

BRUSSELS SPROUTS 'TROIKA'

Brussels sprouts are a cool-season crop that does not do well in really warm climates. This variety gives high yields of firm, rounded sprouts with a good flavour. It has good disease resistance and

Brussels sprouts 'Troika'

120

buds hold well without becoming loose and open. Plants need lots of room to grow; space them 60–75 cm apart. A mature plant may grow 1 m tall. Plant into soil enriched with organic matter. Add a dressing of lime to acid soils before planting and fertilise monthly until sprouts begin to form. High nitrogen fertiliser added after sprouts start to form may result in loose, overblown buds.
SEASON: Sow late summer to autumn. From seed to harvest takes 16–18 weeks.

CABBAGE

Cabbage is adaptable to a wide range of climates and soils, although acid soils must be limed before planting. Forms range from the round ball type through to tall conical types. Large cabbages should be spaced 60 cm or more while small growers can spaced at 30 cm. Cabbage must be grown rapidly with lots of water and fertiliser. Mulch established plants with organic matter to help retain water and nutrients. Cabbages are susceptible to attack from cabbage moth, cabbage white butterfly and aphids.
SEASON: Sow from early spring through to autumn. From seed to harvest takes 14–16 weeks.

Cabbage 'Castello Fl'

From the Little Wonders range, this excellent hybrid cabbage produces heads that can be harvested when about 8 cm in diameter or allowed to grow on to full size. Ideal for small gardens, it can also be grown in large containers with plants spaced about 15 cm apart. It is very resistant to splitting or running to seed even when left to mature to full size.

Cabbage 'Savoy King Fl'

This first-class Savoy-type cabbage produces large solid heads of dark green, crinkly leaves. Plants are vigorous and uniform in size. Flavour is excellent.

Cabbage 'Sugarloaf'

This variety has large, dense, conical heads. Its shape makes it suitable for fine shredding for salads. Cabbages tend to mature over several weeks, allowing harvesting to be spread over some time.

Cabbage, red cabbage 'Ruby Ball Fl'

Red cabbage is becoming popular for adding colour to salads. This variety forms large solid heads with great colour and has few outer leaves—there is little waste in preparation.

Top left: Cabbage 'Castello F1'. Above left to right: 'Savoy King F1', 'Sugarloaf', red cabbage 'Ruby Ball F1'

CAPSICUM

Capsicums may be sweet and mild flavoured or hot and tangy. They can be grown only in warm conditions and prefer well-drained soil enriched with organic matter. Plants should be spaced about 50 cm apart in the garden. As long as fruit is picked regularly, capsicums will go on bearing until the weather turns cold. In warm areas plants often continue cropping into a second year. Adequate fertiliser and regular watering will ensure well-formed succulent fruit. Plants do best when sheltered from strong wind.
SEASON: Sow in spring to summer. From seed to harvest takes 5–6 months.

Capsicum 'Californian Wonder'

This widely grown sweet pepper has a blocky shape and smooth, shiny green skin at maturity. It can be used green or allowed to ripen further until it is uniformly red.

Capsicum 'Giant Bell'

This large bell-shaped fruit has a mild, sweet flavour. Fruit grow 10–12 cm long and 8 cm wide. It can be eaten green or allowed to mature until it becomes red.

Capsicum 'Jalapeno'

This is a very hot Mexican variety that is harvested when the fruits are about 5 cm

Top left to right: Capsicum 'Californian Wonder'; 'Giant Bell'; 'Jalapeno'. Above left to right: 'Seven Colours' (courtesy of The Digger's Club); 'Sweet Allsorts'; 'Sweet Delight Mixed'

long. It is an excellent variety to cultivate in the home garden. Fruits can be green to red at maturity. Some people prefer to dry these chillies before use. Another good seed selection of hot chillies is packed simply as 'Hot Pepper'.

Capsicum 'Seven Colours'

This selection from the Heirloom seed range contains seed of varieties that produce fruit of purple, orange, green, red, brown or gold. A decorative addition to the vegetable or flower garden, this range will suit balcony gardeners too.

Capsicum 'Sweet Allsorts'

This seed selection will delight and surprise you when the fruits come to maturity. You can expect a wide range of shape and colour but all will be juicy and sweet in flavour.

Capsicum 'Sweet Delight Mixed'

This mix contains mainly red, yellow or green varieties with maybe the occasional purple. Fruits are mostly squat and blocky but very succulent and sweet.

CARROT

Carrots give great value for the small growing space needed. They are eaten raw or cooked and young carrots eaten straight from the garden are a real taste treat. Carrots can be grown in any well-drained soil that is kept weed-free. If the space was fertilised for a previous crop it should not need further treatment. If the soil is extremely poor a small amount of fertiliser could be dug in about a month before sowing. Carrot seed is sown directly where it is to grow and it is easier to sow if the fine seed is mixed with sand. After sowing, cover the seed with a fine layer of soil and then mulch with a very small amount of very old manure or compost to prevent the soil surface from caking, which can prevent

the tiny seedlings from pushing through the surface. Rows should be about 30 cm apart and seedlings can be thinned as they develop. Baby carrots need only 2.5 cm spacings but large growers may need 10 cm spacings. Carrots can be harvested over a long period as some roots can be pulled when they are quite small while the remainder are left in the ground to grow large.

GROWING CARROTS SUCCESSFULLY

To reduce the risk of carrots developing forked, misshapen roots, don't fertilise the bed just before you sow. Also be sure to work the soil well before planting carrots in order to remove stones and clods of earth that might cause forking.

Keep the soil evenly moist during the growing season to prevent carrots with cracked roots—roots crack when heavy rain or irrigation occurs after a prolonged dry spell.

Make sure the crown of the root is kept covered with soil to avoid greening of tops. Excess top growth usually occurs when you apply too much high-nitrogen fertiliser.

Carrots may bolt or run to seed when a cool spell occurs during the early growth period, while the soft growth of new seedlings may shrivel or burn on hot sunny days during the early stages of growth. It is important to keep the plants adequately watered.

A pale colour may simply be a feature of the variety or it may be a sign that the soil is too acid. Add lime to the soil and feed the plants with balanced fertiliser during growth.

Top left to right: Carrot 'All Year Round'; 'Amsterdam Forcing 3–Minicor'. Centre left to right: 'Baby Pak'; 'Chantenay Red Cored'; 'Earlybird'. Above left to right: 'Navarre F1'; 'Newmarket F1'; 'Topweight Improved'

SEASON: Carrots can be sown from late winter through to autumn. For full-size roots it takes about 18–20 weeks from seed to maturity, less for some varieties.

Carrot 'All Year Round'

Fine colour and long, pointed roots are features of this popular variety. This variety stores well and harvesting can be at whatever stage suits the gardener.

Carrot 'Amsterdam Forcing 3–Minicor'

From the Little Wonders range, this is a sweet, crunchy carrot that can be harvested when roots are only 1.5 cm in diameter. They can be eaten raw or cooked whole. They may also be left in the garden to mature further.

Carrot 'Baby Pak'

This small, blunt-ended carrot can be harvested after 9–10 weeks. They are at their best when roots are 10 cm long.

Carrot 'Chantenay Red Cored'

Thick, rather stumpy roots are a feature of this variety. Colour is a rich orange and its fine texture is ideal for slicing. This is an ideal variety for shallow soils.

Carrot 'Earlybird'

Adaptable to even heavier soils, this variety bears excellent crops of long, smooth roots. It has a very sweet flavour.

Carrot 'Navarre F1'

This vigorous hybrid carrot produces long, cylindrical roots that are of great uniformity. Smooth skin and sweet flavour make it a delight to grow.

Carrot 'Newmarket F1'

A feature of this fine hybrid carrot is that top growth is strong, aiding good development and easy pulling. Sweet, slightly tapered roots have a bright uniform colour.

Carrot 'Topweight Improved'

This is an old favourite grown both commercially and in the home garden. It is resistant to virus disease and produces long, tapering roots of first-class flavour.

CAULIFLOWER 'QUICKHEART'

This is a fine variety of cauliflower that forms a compact, white head of flower known as the curd. Heads of this strain remain firm over a longer period than in some other varieties. Cauliflowers do best on well-drained soils containing some lime or dolomite. Space cauliflowers 60–75 cm apart each way and plant firmly. When plants are about half grown soil can be hilled slightly around the base to prevent wind damage. The heads should be clean and white at maturity but they can be discoloured by sun, rain, frost or dust and so protection is needed once the leaves open out to expose them. Outside leaves can be snapped at the midrib and tucked over the head for protection or tied loosely together to form a tent.

SEASON: Sow seed from midsummer to autumn. From seed to harvest takes from 16 to 20 weeks.

Cauliflower 'Quickheart'

CELERY 'CRISP AND CRUNCHY'

Celery must be grown quickly to prevent stalks from becoming tough and stringy. It needs rich soil with a high organic content and plenty of water. As long as soil drains well it is almost impossible to overwater celery. Grow this compact, self-blanching variety in blocks with plants spaced no more than 25 cm apart to aid blanching. Plants on the outside of the block will be greener than those in the centre. Remove any side shoots to maintain the density of the bunch.
SEASON: Sow from spring to autumn. From seed to harvest takes 20–24 weeks.

CHICORY 'CRYSTAL HEAD'

Easy to grow, this chicory produces a crisp lettuce-like head with a conical shape. Grown quickly it has no bitter taste like many forms of chicory. Rich soil with a high organic content and plenty of water will produce an excellent crop. Unlike some other forms of chicory and endive this variety needs no blanching. Space plants 10 cm apart.
SEASON: Sow from spring through to autumn. From seed to maturity takes from 10 to 12 weeks.

CHILLI

See Capsicum (pages 122–3).

CHINESE CABBAGE 'NAGAOKA 60 DAYS F1'

Used in salads and stir fries or cooked like cabbage, this quick-growing vegetable has a crisp texture and a slight mustard-like tang. This hybrid variety will produce crops of great uniformity and vigour. Plants must be grown without check by planting into well-limed soil high in organic matter. Ample, regular water must be given. Sow seed where it is to grow and thin out to 30 cm spacings.
SEASON: Sow late summer to autumn. From seed to harvest takes 8–10 weeks.

CHINESE MUSTARD

A popular vegetable for use in salads and stir fries, this has a strong peppery flavour. Use only young leaves in salads. If plants run to seed the flavour becomes hotter and stronger. Grow it in well-limed soil enriched with manure or compost and give regular watering to produce the crop quickly. Seeds are sown direct into the ground where they are to grow and are thinned to 15 cm spacings.

Left to right: Celery 'Crisp and Crunchy'; chicory 'Crystal Head'; Chinese cabbage 'Nagaoka 60 Days F1'

Left to right: Chinese mustard; chopsuey greens 'Shungiku'; cress 'Fine Curled'

SEASON: Sow from summer through to early autumn. Leaves can be picked 8–12 weeks after sowing.

CHOPSUEY GREENS 'SHUNGIKU'

The young leaves may be added to salads but are usually stir fried. It must be grown quickly to ensure sweet, tender leaves. Plant into well-drained soil enriched with manure or compost. Plenty of water is needed during hot or very dry weather but never let plants become waterlogged. Space plants 30–40 cm apart.

SEASON: Seed can be sown throughout the year except during summer. Leaves can be ready for harvest in 4–6 weeks.

CRESS 'FINE CURLED'

Cress can be grown indoors or out. It has been used as a salad green since the time of the ancient Romans. Cress is often combined with mustard. Indoors, seed can be sown on seed-raising mix or moist cotton wool. Seedlings must be given plenty of bright light so that they grow strong and green. Outdoors it is best grown in shallow trays rather than in the garden. Seedlings must be kept very well watered. Cress can be picked as needed but is mostly cut at 5–10 cm high; do so often enough to prevent flowering.

SEASON: Seed can be sown year round. It can be cut after 3–4 weeks.

CUCUMBER

Crisp cucumbers add a refreshing taste to summer salads and sandwiches. Strictly warm-season growers, cucumbers need plenty of water. If space is limited, grow bush types; you could also train vines up a trellis where little space is needed at ground level. Prepare soil by digging in lots of decayed manure or compost plus complete fertiliser. Sow 4–5 seeds in a group and later thin to retain only 2–3 of the strongest seedlings. Seed is easy to handle and can be sown where it is to grow. Space plants about 90 cm apart. A cucumber will only set as many fruit as can be brought to maturity so it is natural for some surplus to turn yellow and drop off at an early stage. Once vines start cropping, fruit must be picked regularly before it becomes over-mature.

SEASON: Sow seed in spring and summer. Fruit will be ready to pick in 8–12 weeks.

Cucumber 'Armenian'

From the Heirloom range comes this long, fleshy fruit that may grow from 60 to 90 cm. The flesh is pale green and the outer skin distinctly ribbed.

Cucumber 'Burpless F1'

With a sweet flavour and juicy texture the variety 'Burpless F1' is the right choice for those people who suffer from indigestion after eating cucumbers. If you intend to use it in salads you should pick the fruit when it is about 20–25 cm in length.

Cucumber 'Crystal Apple'

This cucumber can be grown along the ground but it is often grown as a climber supported by trellis or wire. Fruits are cream to palest yellow-green and are at their peak when they are about tennis-ball size. This variety is well suited to container growing.

SOWING FLAT SEEDS

You should sow all flat seeds such as cucumber, marrow and pumpkin on edge in order to reduce the risk of rotting.

Top left to right: Cucumber 'Armenian' (courtesy The Digger's Club); 'Burpless F1', 'Crystal Apple'. Centre left to right: 'Lebanese'; 'Long Green Supermarket'; 'Pickling Gherkin'. Above left: 'Spacemaster'

Cucumber 'Lebanese'

This sweet-flavoured fruit is eaten whole or sliced without peeling. Flesh is pale green. This is also a 'burpless' variety. Best picked when not much more than 10 cm long, it crops very well as long as fruit is harvested regularly.

Cucumber 'Long Green Supermarket'

A very reliable variety, this produces good crops of straight, uniform fruits of excellent flavour. It is most often used for slicing or dicing in salads. Pick fruits when they are about 20 cm long.

Cucumber 'Pickling Gherkin'

Although described as a pickling gherkin this can also be allowed to grow full size for use in salads. For pickling, harvest fruits when they are between 5 and 10 cm long. This is a heavy cropping variety.

Cucumber 'Spacemaster'

This is a compact bush type of cucumber that can be grown in containers or in the garden. Despite its smaller growth it produces high yields of tasty fruit. Space plants 50 cm apart in the garden.

EGGPLANT 'BLACK BEAUTY'

Eggplant or aubergines can only be grown in warm conditions. Plants grow to almost 1 m high and so should be grown in a sheltered position. Soil must drain freely and be well prepared by digging in complete fertiliser and manure or compost before sowing. Seeds can be sown in pots or trays and transplanted when 10–15 cm high. Space plants 60–75 cm apart. Plants yield from five to eight fruit per plant. Fruit should be harvested when well formed and the skin is dark purple, smooth and shiny. Cut rather than pull fruits from the bush.
SEASON: Sow the seed in spring or summer. From seed to harvest takes 14–16 weeks.

Eggplant 'Black Beauty'

ENDIVE 'RUFFEC GREEN CURLED'

Endive must be grown quickly by planting into rich soil with regular watering and fertilising until harvest. The finely cut, curly leaves are slightly bitter but this is reduced if outer leaves are tied together over the plant or the whole plant covered with a pot for a few days. This blanches the leaves which will taste milder. Space plants 20–25 cm apart.
SEASON: Ideally sown in late summer to autumn, it can also be sown from spring through summer. From seed to maturity takes 8–12 weeks.

Endive 'Ruffec Green Curled'

Left to right: Kale 'Dwarf Green Curled'; kohlrabi 'Purple Vienna'; lamb's lettuce 'Jade'

GARLIC CHIVES
See Chives (pages 106–7).

KALE 'DWARF GREEN CURLED'
Also known as borecole, this winter vegetable is closely related to cabbage and Brussels sprouts and is simply and best described as a non-heading variety of cabbage. The very curly leaves are dark blue-green. It is a very hardy vegetable, withstanding very cold conditions. Leaves can be harvested like silver beet, which will encourage new growth, or the whole plant can be cut off at ground level. It is grown and eaten like cabbage. Grow in any well-drained soil that has had lime or dolomite added. Plants should be spaced 35–45 cm apart.
SEASON: Sow from spring to autumn. Harvest leaves after 7–8 weeks.

KOHLRABI 'PURPLE VIENNA'
Described as having a taste midway between a turnip and cabbage, kohlrabi enjoys the same growing conditions. The part eaten is actually the swollen stem base. 'Purple Vienna' is a traditional variety that has been in cultivation for a very long time. It is eaten cooked or grated raw in salads. To enjoy the best flavour and texture, harvest roots when they are the size of a tennis ball or less.

Plants need well-drained soil that has been limed and enriched with organic matter. To ensure that roots will be tender, grow plants rapidly with regular applications of fertiliser and plenty of water. Final plant spacings should be about 20 cm apart.
SEASON: Sow from spring through to autumn. Harvesting can begin from 8 to 10 weeks after sowing although it may take 12–14 weeks to full maturity.

LAMB'S LETTUCE 'JADE'
An unusual vegetable to add a different flavour to salads, lamb's lettuce is also known as corn salad. Some describe its distinctive taste as nutty. The shiny leaves are best picked young and individually to allow plants to continue growing. It can be grown in any well-drained soil but preferably one that has been enriched with organic matter. To ensure tender, flavoursome leaves, keep plants growing quickly with regular applications of liquid fertiliser. It does best in full sun but will tolerate shade for part of the day. Seed can be sown direct and seedlings later thinned to about 10 cm spacings.
SEASON: Sow during spring and summer. The first leaves will be ready for picking in 8 weeks.

LEEK

Leeks are the easiest member of the onion family to cultivate. They grow in any well-drained soil. Seed can be sown in trays and later transplanted or planted direct, the seedlings later being thinned to about 10 cm intervals. Transplant seedlings when they reach 20 cm high, into holes about 15 cm deep. Deep planting helps blanch the lower stems. Keep plants growing quickly with regular water and fertiliser and keep the area weed-free. Stems can also be blanched by tying cardboard or several thicknesses of newspaper around the plants.

SEASON: Sow seed from spring to autumn. Time to harvest depends on the size required but the first stems should be ready after 12–14 weeks. Full-size leeks take from 16 to 20 weeks.

Leek 'Lyon Prizetaker'

This early maturing variety can produce very large stems when given plenty of water and high-nitrogen fertiliser. This strain can be grown to a large size without losing its texture or flavour.

Leek 'Poristo'

From the Little Wonders range, this is a small, solid leek that can be harvested when stems are 2 cm thick or less. They have great flavour and are ideal for small gardens or for container growing. The first stems can be picked about 9 weeks after sowing.

LETTUCE

Lettuces more than almost any other vegetable must be grown quickly so that hearts and leaves are crisp and juicy. Lettuces can be grown year-round but most varieties will not tolerate really hot conditions. It is important to choose the right variety for the time of year and to prepare the soil well before planting. Sow a few seeds at a time over several weeks to ensure a continuity of supply. Many lettuces can be successfully grown in containers or a small area of ground. Prepare the soil by digging in large amounts of decayed manure or compost and spreading fertiliser along the sides of trenches where the seeds are to be sown. Refill the trenches and plant the seeds into a groove 5–10 mm deep. Firm the soil, mulch lightly and water in. Once seedlings have emerged, give regular water and apply liquid fertiliser every 10–14 days.

SEASON: Depends on variety. Most can be sown in spring or autumn, some year round. From seed to harvest takes 8–10 weeks.

Left and right: Leek 'Lyon Prizetaker'; 'Poristo'

LETTUCE MATURITY

Different types of lettuce will mature at different rates. The loose leaf lettuce varieties are quickest to mature, while the hearting types will take longer.

Top left to right: Lettuce 'All Year Round'; 'Great Lakes'; 'Green Cos'. Centre left to right: 'Green Mignonette'; 'Ice Cube'; 'Lollo Rossa'. Above left to right: 'Mixed Salad Leaves'; 'Red & Green Salad Bowl Mixed'; 'Saladin'

Lettuce 'All Year Round'
This solid, hearting lettuce can be sown any time of year. It is adaptable to a range of conditions and is very hardy.

Lettuce 'Great Lakes'
This variety grows well through the warmer weather without running to seed. It forms a large, crisp head.

Lettuce 'Green Cos'
Forming large conical heads of crisp leaves, cos lettuce has good flavour and texture. Sow in spring or autumn to be ready for harvest in 8 weeks.

Lettuce 'Green Mignonette'
This lettuce is ideal for tossed salads as all but the outside leaves can be used. Flavour is good right through to the small, loose hearts. This can be sown any time except winter.

Lettuce 'Ice Cube'
The small, firm heads of these lettuces from the Little Wonders range can be harvested when only 7–8 cm in diameter. Individual leaves can also be picked in the early stages of growth. It may also be left to grow on to full size but is most popular for use as a mini lettuce.

Lettuce 'Lollo Rossa'
Frilled leaves with red margins make this lettuce variety a must for visual appeal. Individual leaves can be picked as needed too. This plant can be grown most times of the year except midsummer.

Lettuce 'Mixed Salad Leaves'
If you want salads every day then this is the seed mix for you. This is a blend of several different types of lettuce with a range of colour and leaf shape. Individual leaves can be harvested as needed and the plants will keep producing more. Sow in spring or summer.

Lettuce 'Red & Green Salad Bowl Mixed'
Another seed mix fit for the ornamental garden, this is a range of non-hearting lettuces. These loose-leaf lettuces are of the oak-leaf type with a pretty leaf shape. Seed can be sown in spring or autumn.

Lettuce 'Saladin'
Forming large, dark green, crisp heads 'Saladin' does best in slightly cool conditions. Seed can be sown from late summer through autumn or in cold districts in late winter or spring.

MARROW 'LONG GREEN BUSH 2'
Closely related to zucchini and cucumber, marrow are traditionally stuffed with savoury meats and spices and roasted. This is a popular variety to grow as it forms a compact, bushy plant suitable for the smaller garden or container. Cropping will continue over a long period if the first picking is made after 8–10 weeks. Younger marrows are sweeter and more tender than large, oversized ones. Like all cucurbits, marrows are strictly warm-season vegetables and seeds should be sown in groups of 3–4 about 90 cm apart. Keep plants growing vigorously with plenty of water and fertiliser. Grow in a well-drained soil enriched with organic matter.
SEASON: Sow in spring and summer. The main crop takes 10–16 weeks from seed to harvest, depending on the desired size.

Marrow 'Long Green Bush 2'

MELON

Delicious melons are summer favourites.
They need plenty of space to grow but as
long as they have plenty of sun and water
they are easy to grow. Before planting,
enrich the soil with lots of organic
matter. Plant seeds in groups of 4–5 at
intervals of 50 cm. Allow 1 m between
rows if a number of vines are being
planted. When seedlings are growing
well, thin out to the strongest two in
each group. Keep the area weed-free and
mulch with manure, compost or straw.
Keep the vines growing strongly with
plenty of water to ensure sweet, juicy
melons. Powdery mildew can be a
problem in humid conditions.
SEASON: Sow seed during spring and
summer. From seed to harvest takes
12–14 weeks.

Rock melon 'Hales Best'

This tasty rock melon has been popular
for years as it has a good flavour and is
also resistant to powdery mildew. The
fruit is large and rounded with pale
orange flesh. Ripe rock melon has a
delicious fragrance.

Rock melon 'Planters Jumbo'

This newer variety of rock melon
produces large fruits that are ribbed on
the outside. The flavour is excellent and
the flesh of 'Planters Jumbo' is a deep
reddish orange colour.

Watermelon 'Candy Red'

Large-fruited watermelons like this are a
thirst quenching summer favourite.
Individual fruits may weigh up to 12 kg.
The pale green skin encloses juicy, deep
red flesh. Watermelons are ripe when the
underneath turns yellow and the melon
gives a hollow sound when it is tapped.

Watermelon 'Sugar Baby'

This is good choice for those who cannot
use huge watermelons as the round fruits
of this variety grow from 15 to 20 cm in
diameter and weigh only about 4 kg. Skin
is dark green, encasing sweet, deep pink
flesh that has few seeds.

Top left: Rock melon 'Hales Best'. Above left to right: Rock melon 'Planters Jumbo'; watermelon 'Candy Red'; watermelon 'Sugar Baby'

Mustard 'White'

Okra 'Clemson's Spineless'

MUSTARD 'WHITE'

Mustard is quickly and easily grown indoors and out. It has a slightly peppery taste. Mustard grows more quickly than cress and should be sown four days later if you want to pick them at the same time. Indoors, seed can be sprinkled onto cotton wool or seed-raising mix and kept moist at all times. Outdoors, sow in shallow trays of seed-raising mix and keep damp. Seed will germinate in a few days in warm weather. There is no need to thin seedlings as the leaves are cut at 5–10 cm high. Sow seed every few weeks for a continuous supply.

SEASON: Sow seed all year round. Plants will be ready for harvest in about 4 weeks.

OKRA 'CLEMSON'S SPINELESS'

Known as lady's fingers, okra is related to hibiscus and produces yellow hibiscus-like flowers. It needs very warm conditions to do well and grow quickly. Plants may grow about 1 m high and so should be planted in a sheltered spot. Okra is used to flavour and thicken stews, soups and curries. Pods must be picked 4–5 days after the flowers have opened to be tender and sweet. Regular picking every couple of days ensures that pods are not left to become tough and stringy.

Space seedlings 40–50 cm apart. Plant into soil enriched with organic matter and keep plants growing quickly with regular water and feeding. This variety is reliable and gives vigorous cropping in as little as 8 weeks in the tropics.

SEASON: Sow seed in spring to early summer. In most areas from seed to harvest takes 14–16 weeks.

ONION

Onions have been cultivated for many thousands of years. It is possibly the most universally grown vegetable crop in the world. Onions come in a variety of shapes with skin colours that include white, brown and reddish purple. It is important to grow the variety that suits the season or results may be poor. The main onion crops are grown through winter into spring but some varieties can be grown at other seasons. Onions take a long time to mature but with the right handling many types can be stored for a long time. Onions for storing should not be pulled until the tops have turned brown and fallen over. They must then be spread on racks to dry properly before they are cleaned and stored. Spring onions, shallots and bunching onions are grown to be used fresh and cannot be stored for any length of time.

Onions like a well-limed soil rich in organic matter. You may need to add lime or dolomite to the soil before planting. Dig trenches 10–15 cm wide and 5 cm deep and then band fertiliser along the sides of the trench. Refill the trench and sow the seed into a shallow groove in the centre. Seedlings can be raised in boxes or trays but direct sowing saves double handling. Final spacings should have plants about 10 cm apart with 30 cm between rows. Thinnings can be chopped up and used to flavour or garnish food.

SEASON: This varies according to type. Many onions are sown in autumn to early winter and will take 6 or 7 months to mature. Shallots will take from 8 to 12 weeks from seed to harvest.

ONION VARIETIES

Onions are a crop sensitive to day length or the amount of light they receive, so it is important to choose the correct variety and sow seed at the right time. If varieties are sown out of season, plants will not thrive and will not produce bulbs.

Early varieties such as 'Hunter River Brown' are 'short-day' onions. Others such as 'Californian Red', 'Odourless' and 'Creamgold' are mid-season varieties.

In warm northern latitudes such as Brisbane, sow early varieties from late summer to late autumn. In latitudes such as Sydney or Perth, sow early varieties in autumn and sow mid-season ones in winter. In colder and southern latitudes such as southern Victoria, Tasmania and Mt Gambier, sow early and mid-season varieties in succession from autumn to early spring.

Onion 'Creamgold'

This variety has light brown, medium sized, globe-shaped bulbs and pungent flesh. Described as a mid-season onion, it has excellent keeping qualities. Sow in autumn to early winter.

Onion 'Early Californian Red'

Red onions tend to have a slightly milder flavour than brown onions. They make a popular addition to salads as their colour adds visual appeal. These onions are a flattened globe shape with a fine red colour. Sow in autumn.

Onion 'Hunter River Brown'

An all-round, early-maturing onion, this variety has been popular for many years and is considered by many to be the best of the early onions. The large globe-shaped bulb has a pale brown skin. It keeps well and has a strong pungent flavour. Sow in autumn.

Onion 'Odourless'

With a slightly flattened shape and a pale brown skin this is truly an odourless onion that stores very well. This is a mid-season onion that should be sown in autumn to early winter.

Onion 'Creamgold'

Top left to right: Onion 'Early Californian Red', 'Hunter River Brown', 'Odourless'. Centre left to right: Onion 'Pickling–Paris Silverskin', shallot 'Ambition F1', shallot 'Longwhite Bunching'. Above left to right: Spring onion 'Bunching Onion–Ishikura', 'Redmate', 'White Lisbon'

Onion 'Pickling–Paris Silverskin'

Often described as a cocktail onion, this is a sweet, white pickling onion that is ready for harvest in 8–12 weeks. Its crisp white flesh makes it ideal for salads and sandwiches too. It can be sown year round and so successive sowings can be made over several weeks to ensure a plentiful and regular supply.

Shallot 'Ambition F1'

True shallots are like small onions that grow as a bunch of bulbs. This fine, vigorous grower yields flavoursome bulbs with a sweet nutty taste. Bulbs can be used green, before they are fully matured, in salads or allowed to mature fully to be dried and stored like other large onions. The green leaves can be chopped and used in salads and bulbs can also be pickled. Sow seed from autumn through to early winter.

Shallot 'Longwhite Bunching'

This is the type of shallot familiar to most people as an ingredient in salads. The leaves can be chopped and used like chives and the long, white stalks can be used in many dishes. Most of the plant can be eaten with little waste. This is a quick-growing crop that matures in as little as 8–12 weeks. It can be sown year round and so successive sowings can be made to ensure a continuous supply.

Spring onion 'Bunching Onion–Ishikura'

'Ishikura' is an excellent type of salad onion that has a long white stem and blue-green leaves. Most of the plant can be eaten with little waste. The flavour is first class and although this spring onion can be ready to harvest in 8–12 weeks it can be left to grow thicker stems without losing its distinctive taste. This plant can be sown year round—so it is worth making space for this versatile vegetable in your garden.

Spring onion 'Redmate'

With a mild flavour and crisp flesh this red-skinned spring onion from the Little Wonders range will create great interest. It is used in salads and stir fries, adding both flavour and colour, and the green tops can be chopped and used like chives. Spring onions can be harvested at whatever stage suits your needs. This variety can be sown year round and pencil-thick stems will be ready for harvest in 8–12 weeks. It can be left to mature and form bulbs.

Spring onion 'White Lisbon'

This is an ideal salad onion as it has a mild flavour. It forms a small bulb below the long neck and most of the plant can be eaten. Young, tender tops can be used like chives and the stems and bulbs are chopped or used whole in salads and stir fries. This variety can be sown year round with young stems ready for harvest in 8–12 weeks. Make several sowings a few weeks apart to provide a continuous supply of spring onions.

PAK CHOI

Also known as Bok Choi or Chinese chard, this is familiar to all lovers of Chinese food as a major ingredient in several dishes. The outer leaves with their

Pak choi

thick, white midribs are chopped and braised or stir fried. The inner leaves are sometimes used chopped in salads if they are very young and tender. It needs the same growing conditions as cabbage, namely a well-limed soil rich in organic matter and plenty of water to maintain rapid growth. Seed is sown directly where it is to grow. Plants should be spaced 20–30 cm apart. It is very easy to grow and will be ready to harvest in just a few weeks.

SEASON: Sow seed in summer and autumn, also spring in cool districts. Harvest bunches in 6–8 weeks.

PARSLEY

See pages 109–10.

PARSNIP

Parsnips need much the same growing conditions as carrots. They do not take up much space and give a good return for the space they occupy. Although adaptable to a range of soils, parsnips will do best in free-draining soils that have been well dug. Do not incorporate manure or fertiliser into the soil immediately before planting as this can cause the parsnips to fork or become distorted. Sow the seed, mixed with sand, along a shallow groove and lightly cover with soil. Apply a very thin layer of old manure or compost over the surface to prevent the soil surface caking. Tiny seedlings cannot push through a crusted soil. Once the seedlings are growing strongly, thin them out to 20–25 cm spacings. Keep the area weed-free. Make sure your parsnip seed is fresh as you will only achieve poor results from old seed. Pull the roots at the size you prefer but make sure you do so before the plants run to seed.

SEASON: Seed can be sown year round except in winter. From seed to harvest takes 20–24 weeks.

Parsnip 'Arrow'

This tasty parsnip comes from the Little Wonders range. It bears long narrow topped roots and is suitable for harvesting as a mini vegetable; however, it can also be allowed to grow on to full size. If you are growing this parsnip as a small variety the plants can be spaced 15 cm apart.

Parsnip 'Hollow Crown'

Probably the most commonly grown of all parsnips, 'Hollow Crown' produces good compact conical roots. Roots can be pulled from 18 weeks on depending on personal preference.

Left to right: Parsnip 'Arrow'; 'Hollow Crown'

SOWING RADISH WITH PARSNIP

Parsnip can take a little while to germinate. It is a good idea to mix parsnip and radish seed together so that the faster growing radish will mark the rows.

PEA

Peas grow best in slightly cool conditions but will not tolerate frost. Frost during flowering will damage or kill the flowers, causing the loss of the crop. Many peas grow quite tall and need the support of trellis or wire, but some small-growing varieties can be grown without support. Growing plants against a support means that they take up less room at ground level. Peas can be grown in all climatic zones but planting must be timed to suit the climate. They do best on well-drained soil with a good, open structure. If the soil is very acid add lime or dolomite before planting. Sow seed into moist soil where it is to grow, at 5 cm intervals. Cover with soil, firm down and water lightly. Peas sown into moist soil should not need watering again until seedlings emerge—overwatering will rot the seed in the ground. Keep the growing area free of weeds. Once plants are cropping, pick pods every few days so plants continue to flower and set pods. After the plants have finished cropping dig in the spent plants as they will help to provide nitrogen for a following crop. In warm weather they will rot down quite quickly, especially if the soil is kept damp. In mild, humid conditions peas can be attacked by powdery mildew.

SEASON: Sow peas from autumn through to spring. Most peas will take 12–16 weeks from seed to harvest although a few will crop more quickly.

Top left to right: Pea 'Dwarf Blue Bantam'; 'Early Crop Massey'; 'Greenfeast'.
Above left to right: 'Oregon Dwarf Snow Pea'; 'Sugar Snap'; 'Telephone'

Pea 'Dwarf Blue Bantam'

This large-podded pea is very quick to mature, producing a crop in as little as 8–10 weeks from seed. Plants will grow from 40 to 50 cm high. Growing stems can be supported with sticks or twigs to keep them off the ground.

Pea 'Early Crop Massey'

Ready to pick in 12–14 weeks, this is a popular early dwarf variety. It will grow about 60 cm high and produce a good crop of sweet, well-filled pods. It is sometimes known as 'Melbourne Market'.

Pea 'Greenfeast'

One of the main types of pea grown, this is a strong, reliable grower that should reach about 70 cm in height. It yields extremely well and adapts well to a range of both soil and weather conditions.

Pea 'Oregon Dwarf Snow Pea'

Snow peas provide both great flavour and nutrition with economy as the whole pod is eaten. Pods are picked while they are still quite flat but if they are left on the bush they will continue to develop like normal peas. Growing about 50 cm high, this variety is a heavy cropper.

Pea 'Sugar Snap'

When picked young these peas can be treated like beans—slice them or cook them whole to provide a delicious tasting vegetable. If allowed to mature further, the pod can be cooked whole but should be 'stringed'. Pods are also delicious used raw in salads. This is a tall grower to about 1.8 m and so needs support.

Pea 'Telephone'

This tall grower is probably the most popular of all the climbing peas. It will grow to about 1.8 m and so needs support. It bears tasty, full pods that can be picked over a long period.

POTATOES

Potatoes are not grown from true seed but from seed tubers. They do take up a lot of space but they are easy to grow and generally bear heavy crops. Seed potatoes are usually available from nurseries in late winter and spring. In mild areas where a second crop is often planted in late summer, certified stock will probably not be available so it will be necessary to save some good potatoes from the spring crop. Buy certified disease-free tubers and plant about 15 cm deep and 30 cm apart. The soil should be well dug over before planting and must drain well. Do not plant potatoes on soil that has been recently limed as this may predispose the crop to potato scab, a fungal disease. Give the growing plants plenty of water and keep the ground weed-free. When plants start flowering, hill up the soil around the base of the plants to prevent greening of developing potatoes. Small 'new' potatoes can be dug from 4 weeks after flowering. These must be used quickly as they do not store well. Mature potatoes will store well in a dark, airy place.

SEASON: Sow the main crop of seed potatoes in spring. In mild areas a second crop can be planted in late summer. Time to harvest is 16–20 weeks.

Potatoes

PUMPKIN

Pumpkins are an easy crop to grow during warm weather and if harvested when fully mature can be stored and used over several months. Most vines take up a lot of space but there are some smaller growing bush varieties that are well worth growing. All the smaller types of pumpkin can be grown and trained alongside a trellis in order to save space. Pumpkins for storage must be left on the vines, at least until the stalk has withered and turned brown or preferably until the vine itself is almost dead. Only unblemished, perfectly dry fruits can be stored. Pumpkins must be grown in full sun in free-draining soil that has been enriched with organic matter. Sow the large seeds where they are to grow in groups of 4–6, later removing all but the two or three strongest seedlings. Allow at least 50 cm between groups of seed and 1 m between rows. Keep the vines well watered and mulch around the root zones with manure or compost.

SEASON: Sow seed in spring or summer. From seed to maturity takes from 16 to 20 weeks.

Pumpkin 'Butternut'

'Butternut' pumpkin is pear-shaped with creamy yellow skin and fine textured orange flesh. There is little waste with this pumpkin as the seed cavity is very small. It stores well and the vines give a good yield.

Pumpkin 'Golden Nugget'

This is a delicious tasting pumpkin with deep orange skin and bright orange flesh.

TRANSPLANTING PUMPKINS, MELONS AND CUCUMBERS

Like melons, pumpkins, cucumbers and squash resent transplanting—you should therefore sow seed directly into the position where it is to grow in the garden.

Top left: Pumpkin 'Butternut'. Above left to right: 'Golden Nugget'; 'Jarrahdale'; 'Queensland Blue'

It can be baked without peeling as the skin is very thin. A single plant of this bush type can be grown in a large tub and trained up wire or trellis. It will store well if fully mature when picked.

Pumpkin 'Jarrahdale'
This is a popular variety with home growers. The thin grey skin cuts well and the mid-orange flesh is tasty. Mature pumpkins may weigh up to 5 kg. These can be stored for long periods.

Pumpkin 'Queensland Blue'
Renowned for its good eating qualities, this is a large, green to grey skinned pumpkin. Although the tough skin may be hard to remove, the flavour is first class. Vines yield well, bearing 5–7 kg pumpkins in ideal conditions. It is a very good keeper.

RADICCHIO 'PALLA ROSSA'
A red-leaved radicchio, 'Palla Rossa' forms tight, round heads of crisp leaves. This will add both colour and a slightly bitter tang to salads. It grows best through cool weather and must be grown quickly with plenty of water and fertiliser to avoid excess bitterness in the leaves. It is grown the same way as lettuce. Prepare the soil well by digging in plenty of decayed

organic matter before planting. Sow the seed where it is to grow, later thinning plants to allow 30 cm spacings between both rows and plants.
SEASON: Sow seed in autumn to spring. From seed to harvest takes 10–12 weeks.

RADISH
Growing radishes is very satisfying as they are the quickest vegetable crop of all, some being ready for harvest in as little as 3–4 weeks. Radishes may be small and round or long and tapered. Although there are a number of colours grown, the red or white or red and white types seem the most popular. Radishes are used raw in salads and some varieties, especially the long white types, are popular in Asian cooking. Radishes are so quick that it is worth sowing small amounts of seed every few weeks rather than a great deal at one time. They must be grown quickly to ensure crisp, tasty roots. Prepare the soil by digging in plenty of organic matter and once seeds have germinated give them plenty of water and fertiliser. Rows should be 25 cm apart and seedlings are thinned according to size, generally about 5 cm apart.
SEASON: Sow seed year round. Time to maturity varies with the type grown but many mature in 4–6 weeks.

Radicchio 'Palla Rossa'

HAND POLLINATION
If there is a lack of bees, crops such as melon, pumpkin, cucumber and zucchini will benefit from some help from the gardener. Strip petals from the male flower (the one with no swelling behind the petals) and press the flower against the centre of each female flower. One male pollinates four females. Repeat over 2–3 days at around midday.

Top left and right: Radish 'French Breakfast'; 'Long White Icicle'. Above left to right: 'Mooli'; 'Scarlet Globe'; 'Sparkler'

Radish 'French Breakfast'
Mild flavoured, this is a cylindrical red radish with a white tip. Harvest when young. It usually matures in 4 weeks.

Radish 'Long White Icicle'
This radish is white, long and tapering. It is one of the quickest growers, being ready to eat in 3–4 weeks.

Radish 'Mooli'
White radish is an important vegetable in Asian cooking. 'Mooli' is a long, white radish producing roots up to 30 cm long in good soil. Seedlings should be thinned to 5–8 cm apart. Harvest after 6–9 weeks.

Radish 'Scarlet Globe'
The small, round roots of this radish are bright red and crunchy. Ensure a continuous supply of this easy grower, which matures in 4–6 weeks, by sowing a few seeds every few weeks.

Radish 'Sparkler'
This quick grower has medium-sized round roots that are rich red with white tips. The flavour is excellent. Ready to eat in about 4 weeks from sowing, this is a good variety for container growing.

ROCK MELON
See Melon (page 134).

ROCKET
Rocket is a salad vegetable that adds a peppery bite to plain lettuce salads. Prepare the soil by digging in plenty of organic matter and adding lime or dolomite if the soil tends to be acid. Seed is sown directly into shallow grooves, with seedlings later thinned to allow 20–30 cm between plants. Keep plants well watered and use liquid fertiliser to promote leafy growth. Once plants are growing strongly, pick leaves as required. Cut off flower buds as they appear to prolong the production of leaves.
SEASON: Seed can be sown year round. Leaves should be ready for harvest in about 6 weeks.

SALSIFY 'MAMMOTH SANDWICH IS.'
Also called the vegetable oyster, this vegetable can be boiled, baked, fried or used in creamed soups. Its delicate flavour is said to resemble that of oysters. It must be grown in well-prepared soil that is free draining. No manure or fertiliser should be dug into the soil before planting as this may cause distortion of roots. Seed should be sown where it is to grow with the seedlings later thinned to 10 cm spacings. Water

regularly and keep the area weed-free. Harvest some roots when young, allowing the remainder to become larger.
SEASON: Sow from winter through to autumn. Full-sized roots may take from 20 to 24 weeks to reach maturity.

SHALLOT
See Onion (pages 135–8).

SILVER BEET
Silver beet is easy to grow. Regular picking will promote growth over a long time. Often referred to as spinach, it is not a true spinach but a close relative of beetroot. For good results you must grow this crop in rich soil and provide lots of water and fertiliser. Quick growth ensures tender, tasty leaves. Once plants have developed well, start picking a few leaves from the outside of the clump. Always leave four or five leaves at the centre to allow for quick regrowth. Sow where it is to grow or raise in seed trays and transplant when seedlings are 8–10 cm high. Space plants 30 cm apart in the garden or grow more closely in pots.
SEASON: Sow from spring to early autumn. The first leaves should be ready for harvest in 8–12 weeks.

AVOIDING WASTE
Sowing a whole row of radish or lettuce plants which mature all together at the one time can be a wasteful method of vegetable gardening. The answer is to sow less seed, while also sowing your vegetable seed more often.

Left to right: Rocket; salsify 'Mammoth Sandwich Is.'

Silver beet 'Fordhook Giant'

This is the most popular variety for both home gardeners and commercial growing. It has large, dark green, crinkly leaves and a thick white midrib. It is at its best when picked and cooked straight away.

Silver beet 'Rhubarb Chard'

The long crimson stems add a colourful touch to the vegetable or ornamental garden. It is cooked and eaten like green-stemmed silver beet . As a novelty the red stems can be cut into sections and steamed lightly.

SPINACH

True spinach is a cool-season vegetable that cannot be grown successfully in warm conditions as it will run straight to seed. It is also unusual among vegetables in that it prefers to be grown in partial shade. It does best in free-draining soils that have a high organic content. Like all leafy vegetables it must be grown rapidly with plenty of water and fertiliser to ensure tasty, tender leaves. Plants should be spaced at 30 cm intervals. Once plants are well developed, start picking a few leaves from the outside of the clump but be sure to leave enough in the centre for the plant to regenerate. Spinach is rich in iron and vitamins and can be cooked lightly or the young leaves can be added to salads.

Season: Sow from late summer to early winter. Early spring sowings can be made in cool districts. The first leaves will be ready to pick in 8–12 weeks.

Top: Silver beet 'Fordhook Giant'
Above: 'Rhubarb Chard'

Top: Spinach 'Mazurka F1'
Above: 'Viking'

Spinach 'Mazurka F1'
A good variety for container or garden growing, it produces excellent yields. Plants are resistant to disease and slow to run to seed in warm spells.

Spinach 'Viking'
This is a hardy, vigorous variety in the Little Wonders range, which produces an abundance of dark green leaves. First leaves should be ready for picking in about 8 weeks.

SQUASH 'GREEN BUTTONS F1'
This button squash can be grown successfully in containers or in the garden, but only in warm conditions. It gives a great yield of scalloped lime-green fruits that are very uniform in size. Pick when no more than 5–10 cm in diameter to ensure tenderness and taste. Sow 2–3 seeds where they are to grow in rows about 1 m apart, allowing at least 50 cm between clumps. Thin to leave the two strongest seedlings only. Give plenty of water and fertiliser to maintain rapid growth through the season. It needs well-drained soil rich in organic matter.
SEASON: Sow during spring and summer. From seed to harvest takes 12–14 weeks.

SWEDE 'BEST OF ALL'
Hardy and easily grown, this globe-shaped swede has a purple top over a cream base. The flesh is yellow with a smooth texture and mild flavour. Swedes must be grown in free-draining soil heavily enriched with manure. Seed can be sown direct and later thinned to allow 20–30 cm between plants. Give lots of water during dry periods to ensure roots are tender. In cold weather roots can be left in the ground and dug as needed. Start pulling roots while still small to spread the harvest over several weeks.
SEASON: Sow from late summer through autumn; from late winter to early spring in cold districts. Roots will be ready for harvest in 10–12 weeks.

SWEET CORN
Sweet corn from the garden tastes totally unlike any store-bought corn. It needs room to grow and is best planted in a block to ensure good pollination. Sow where it is to grow, spacing seeds 25 cm apart with the rows 40–50 cm apart. The soil should have a high organic content to help retain moisture. Once plants are about 30 cm high, mulch with manure or compost. Sweet corn must have a regular,

Left to right: Squash 'Green Buttons F1'; swede 'Best of All'

GROWING SWEET CORN
Keep sweet corn roots moist, particularly during the flowering period. Tapping the tassels on the corn will help pollination. Harvest your sweet corn when the silks have turned brown.

plentiful supply of water, and high-nitrogen fertiliser should be applied every three weeks. Keep the ground weed-free but don't disturb the corn roots. Harvest cobs when the silks have just turned brown and are fairly dry; the kernels should be plump and juicy. Test for maturity by pressing a thumbnail into a kernel. If the juice is milky, it is at the perfect stage. If floury dough is exuded, the cob is over-mature and will be tough. Corn earworm is a major pest. To prevent damage clip off the tip of the ear when most of the silks are brown and dry. Cut midway between the top of the cob and the top of the husk.

SEASON: Sow spring to early summer. Harvest cobs in about 12 weeks.

Sweet corn 'Early Extra Sweet F1'

This hybrid has large golden cobs with a sweet flavour. Any other sweet corn planted within a 50 m radius must also be a supersweet variety—if cross-pollination occurs with another variety, eating quality will be variable. If you want to plant several different types of sweet corn, stagger the sowing times by two to three week intervals so that plants will not flower at the same time.

Sweet corn 'Kelvedon Glory F1'

A very reliable variety, this widely grown hybrid corn produces long cobs evenly covered with plump kernels. Although best cooked and eaten right away, sweet corn freezes well.

Sweet corn 'Snow Gold Bicolour F1'

Bicoloured corn is becoming increasingly popular. This is a supersweet variety that produces medium to large cobs with both cream and deep gold kernels. This variety should be grown well away from other sweet corn to avoid cross-pollination.

TOMATO

Home-grown tomatoes have a flavour and texture rarely found in those bought in the supermarket. This is the most often cultivated of all the vegetables. Even people who would rarely consider growing any other vegetable will grow a few tomato plants. There is a great variety of types to grow, even some that are suitable for container growing. Tall varieties may grow to 2 m high while small types may grow to only 40 or 50 cm high. Tomatoes must be grown only in warm conditions. Before planting prepare the soil by digging in animal

Left to right: Sweet corn 'Early Extra Sweet F1', 'Kelvedon Glory F1', 'Snow Gold Bicolour F1'

manure and some complete plant food. Seed can be sown directly into the ground or raised in pots and then transplanted when the seedlings are 10–15 cm high. Space large growers 60–75 cm apart, small growers 45–60 cm apart. For tall varieties put in stakes for support when seedlings are transplanted. As the plant grows, tie it to the stake about every 30 cm with soft twine or budding tape. During growth pinch out the side shoots (laterals) that develop at the junction of the leaf stalks and the main stem. Water plants regularly and deeply, probably twice a week is adequate on most soils. It is important to soak rather than sprinkle to ensure a good deep root system. Ideally allow fruit to ripen fully on the plant. However, fruit that is starting to colour will ripen indoors in a warm spot. Keep the area free of weeds and watch for insect pests. Fruit fly and tomato caterpillar are the worst pests in most areas.

SEASON: Sow seed in spring and summer. From seed to harvest takes 16–20 weeks.

Tomato 'Beefmaster F1'

This is a sturdy hybrid tomato that bears very large uniform fruits. It has good firm texture and good flavour. It is a tall grower that needs staking.

Tomato 'Brasero'

Ideal for container growing, 'Brasero' needs no staking. It has a spreading bushy form and bears masses of small cherry-sized tomatoes that are sweet and juicy. This tomato is part of the Little Wonders range.

Tomato 'Costoluto Florentino'

The large, ribbed fruits of this variety are an Italian favourite. Both texture and outstanding flavour make this tomato ideal for cooking. It can be grown without staking.

Tomato 'Golden Sunrise'

Yellow tomatoes have a sweeter, more subtle flavour than many red types. This heavy cropper produces medium-sized, round fruits.

Tomato 'Grosse Lisse'

Without doubt this is the most popular staking tomato grown in home gardens. This reliable old favourite bears large, succulent, round fruits.

Tomato 'Mortgage Lifter'

Among the best of the heirloom vegetables, this old variety bears large, sweet, ribbed tomatoes. It is very high yielding and a tall grower that needs staking. It is from the Heirloom range.

Tomato 'Oxheart'

This large, solid-fleshed variety has a great flavour. The fruit is smooth skinned with a name that describes its shape. Another old favourite, it is a tall grower that needs staking.

Tomato 'Roma VF'

One of the very best of the so-called egg tomatoes, this very flavoursome tomato is almost seedless. This is the tomato most often used in Italian cooking, especially in sauces and pastes. It will grow tall and need staking.

Tomato 'Rouge de Marmande'

Producing large, tasty, ribbed fruits, this is an early maturing variety that will crop at lower temperatures than most other tomatoes. For this reason it can also be planted later in the season than most varieties. This is a popular older variety.

Tomato 'Sweet 100 F1'

A delicious cherry tomato, this bears prolific crops of sweet, bite-sized fruits. Fruits are produced on long trusses on fairly tall plants and so it needs staking.

Top left to right: Tomato 'Beefmaster F1'; 'Brasero'; 'Costoluto Florentino'. Upper left to right: 'Golden Sunrise'; 'Grosse Lisse'; 'Mortgage Lifter' (courtesy The Digger's Club). Lower left to right: 'Oxheart'; 'Roma VF'; 'Rouge de Marmande'. Above left to right: 'Sweet 100 F1'; 'Tommy Toe' (courtesy The Digger's Club); 'Tropic'

Tomato 'Tommy Toe'
Described as the best tasting of all tomatoes, this heirloom variety produces bright red, smooth fruits about the size of apricots. Plants need staking but have great disease resistance. The seeds are part of Mr Fothergill's Heirloom range.

Tomato 'Tropic'
Although needing support, 'Tropic' can be grown in a pot. Plants are sturdy with good disease resistance. The smooth, globe-shaped fruits are very tasty.

TURNIP 'EARLY PURPLE'
Turnips grow quickly and give good returns for the space they occupy. This variety produces flattened, globe-shaped roots that are cream with a purple flush on top. Flavour is excellent and if the roots are harvested at a young age the flesh is very tender and creamy. Soil should be free draining and heavily enriched with manure before planting. Seed can be sown direct and later thinned to allow 15 cm between plants. Keep the plants growing rapidly with plenty of water, especially in dry or very windy weather. This should ensure that roots are tender and not stringy or tough.

Turnip 'Early Purple'

SEASON: Sow late summer and autumn. Roots will be ready for harvest in 10–12 weeks but can be pulled earlier.

WATERMELON
See Melon (page 134).

ZUCCHINI
Zucchinis, also known as courgettes, like all the other members of the cucurbit family will grow successfully only through the warm months of the year. They normally produce abundant crops as long as harvesting starts from a young stage and picking is frequent and regular. Prepare the soil by digging in plenty of organic matter and add some complete fertiliser to the planting area. Don't overdo the fertiliser or there may be excessive leaf growth at the expense of flowering stems. Sow seeds where they are to grow, singly or in groups of 3–4, later thinning to the two strongest seedlings. Most varieties need plenty of space to spread and so seeds should be spaced about 90 cm apart. Once established, plants must be kept well watered to maintain rapid growth and produce tender fruits. Zucchinis are harvested at an immature stage when they are 10–15 cm long. If the fruit is left on the vine until it grows large it can then be used like marrow. Because of their rapid maturity, several crops can be grown through the season.
SEASON: Sow seed in spring and summer. The first harvesting may be made from 8 to 10 weeks after sowing.

Zucchini 'Ambassador F1'
This small-growing variety from the Little Wonders range may be spaced at 45 cm intervals. It is a fast-maturing variety, producing glossy green fruits that can be harvested once fruits are 8 cm long. This reliable hybrid variety is ideal for small gardens.

Zucchini 'Blackjack'

Probably the best known variety, 'Blackjack' bears prolific crops of very dark green fruits. Bushes are fairly compact and the leaves are spotted with grey patches. In ideal conditions the first harvest may be 7–8 weeks from sowing.

Zucchini 'Gold Rush F.I'

Many people consider the flavour of this gold-skinned variety superior to that of the green-skinned types. A compact grower, this can be grown in containers.

Zucchini 'Greenskin'

This is another variety that produces attractive looking, dark green-skinned fruit. The fruit of this zucchini is a very uniform cylindrical shape.

Zucchini 'Lebanese'

Pale-skinned, mottled fruit with a sweet flavour is characteristic of this variety. It is slightly tear-shaped with a bulbous end. The vines tend to be fairly spreading but very high yielding.

Zucchini 'Moreno F1'

A vigorous growing hybrid, this variety bears prolific crops of dark glossy fruits over a long season. Fruit set is reliable even when there are few pollinating insects around. This variety can be deep frozen for later use.

Top left to right: Zucchini 'Ambassador F1', 'Blackjack', 'Gold Rush F1'. Above left to right: 'Greenskin', 'Lebanese', 'Moreno F1'

PLANTING CHART*

Legend: T = Tropical (yellow), W = Warm (green), C = Cool (blue)

PLANT	SPRING Early	Mid	Late	SUMMER Early	Mid	Late	AUTUMN Early	Mid	Late	WINTER Early	Mid	Late
FLOWERS												
Achillea	C							C	W C	W		
Ageratum	T W C	T W C	T W C	W C	W C	W C	T W	T W	T	T	T	W C
Alstroemeria	W C	W C	C			W C	W C	W	W			
Alyssum	W C	W C	W C	W C	W C	W C	T W	W C	W C	W C	T	
Aquilegia	C				W	W	W C	W C	W C			
Aster	W	W C	W C	W C				T	T			W
Aubrietia								W C	W C	W C		
Balsam	W C	W C	W C	W C							T	W C
Begonia	W C	W C	W C	W					T	T		W C
Bells of Ireland	W C	W C				C	C	W C	W			W
Bidens	W C	W C	W C	W C	W							W
Cabbage, ornamental	C						W	W C	W C	W C		
Calendula	W C						W C	W C	W C	W		C
Californian poppy	W C	W C	W C	W	W							W
Candytuft	W	C	C			C	T W	T W C	W C	W		
Canterbury bells						C	W C	W C	W C	W		
Carnation	T W					W C	W C	T W C	T	T	T	W C
Celosia	T W C	T W C	W C	W C					T	T	T	W
Cineraria						W C	W C	T W C	W C	W C		
Clarkia; godetia	C	C				W C	T W C	T W C	W C	C		
Cleome	W C	W C	W C	W C		T	T	T	T	T		W
Coleus	T W C	T W C	T W C	T W C	W C	W C			T	T	T	W C
Coreopsis	T W C	W C	W C	W			T W	T W C	W C	T	T	T
Cornflower	C		C			W	T W C	T W C	W	T		W
Cosmos; cosmea; cosmidium	T W C	W C	W C	W C	W				T	T	T	T
Dahlia	T W C	W C	W C	W C					T	T		W C
Daisy, English	C	C				W	W C	T W C	W C	W C		
Delphinium	C	C			W C	W C	W	W	W			
Dianthus; pinks	T W C	W C	C			C	T W C	W C	W C	W C	W C	W C
Diascia	W C	C				C	W C	T W C	T W C	W C		
Dimorphotheca	W C	W C	W C	W C						T	T	T
Erigeron	C	C	C			W	W C	W C	W C	W C	T	T
Forget-me-not				C	W C		W C	W	W			
Foxglove				C	W C		W C	W C	W			
Gaillardia	C	C				W	W C	W C	T W C	W C	T	T
Gazania	W C	W C	W C	W					T	T	T	W C
Geranium	T W C	W C	W C	W					T	T	T	W C
Gerbera	W C	W C	W C	W C	T	T	T	T		T	T	W C
Geum	W C	W	W					W	W	W		
Gourd, ornamental	T W	W C	W C	W C					T	T	T	T
Gypsophila	T W C	T W C	W C	W C			T W C	T W C	T W C	T	T	W C
Helichrysum	C	C							W	W C	T	T
Hollyhock				C	W C		W C	W C	W			
Honesty	W C	W					W	W C	W			W
Impatiens	T W C	T W C	W C	T W	C	C	W C	W C	W C	W C	T	W C
Larkspur	C	C				W	W C	W C	W			
Lavatera	C	C	C	C			W	W	W			
Lavender						C	W C	W C	W	W		
Linaria	C	C				W C	T W C	T W C	W C	W C		
Lobelia	C	C				W C	T W C	T W C	W C			

PLANT	SPRING EARLY	SPRING MID	SPRING LATE	SUMMER EARLY	SUMMER MID	SUMMER LATE	AUTUMN EARLY	AUTUMN MID	AUTUMN LATE	WINTER EARLY	WINTER MID	WINTER LATE
Lupin, Russell	🔵	🔵			🔵	🟢🟢	🟢🟢	🟢🟢				
Lychnis						🔵	🟢🟢	🟢🟢	🟢	🟢		
Marigold	🟢🟢	🟢	🟢					🟢	🟡🟡	🟡🟡	🟡🟡	🟡🟡
Mesembryanthemum	🟢	🟢			🟢	🟢🟢🟢	🟢🟢	🟢🟢	🟢🟢			
Mimulus	🔵	🔵🔵	🔵🔵	🔵								🟢
Nasturtium	🟡🟢🟢	🟢🟢	🟢🟢	🟢🟢	🟢	🟢🟢	🟡	🟡	🟡	🟡	🟡	🟡🟡
Nemesia	🔵	🔵				🟢	🟢🟢	🟢🟢	🟢🟢			
Nemophila	🔵	🔵				🟢🟢	🟢🟢🟢	🟢🟢🟢	🟢			
Nigella						🟢🟢	🟢🟢🟢	🟢🟢🟢	🟢🟢			
Nolana	🟡🟢🟢	🟢🟢	🟢🟢	🟢🟢			🟢🟢	🟢🟢	🟢	🟡🟡	🟡	🟡
Pansy	🔵	🔵			🔵🔵	🟢🟢🟢	🟡🟢🟢	🟢🟢🟢	🟢🟢	🟢		
Penstemon	🔵	🔵			🟢	🟢🟢	🟢🟢	🟢🟢				
Petunia	🟢🟢	🟢	🟢🟢	🟢🟢		🟡	🟡	🟡	🟡	🟡		🟡🟡
Phlox	🟢🟢	🟢🟢	🟢🟢	🟢🟢		🟡	🟡	🟡	🟡	🟡		🟡🟡
Poached egg plant	🔵					🟢🟢	🟢🟢	🟢🟢	🟢			
Polyanthus					🔵	🟢🟢	🟢🟢	🟢🟢	🟢			
Poppy					🔵	🟢🟢🟢	🟡🟢🟢	🟢🟢🟢	🟢🟢			
Portulaca	🟡🟢🟢	🟢🟢	🟢🟢	🟢🟢					🟡	🟡	🟡	🟡🟡
Primrose					🔵	🟢🟢	🟢🟢	🟢				
Primula					🔵	🟡🟢🟢	🟢🟢🟢	🟢🟢🟢	🟢🟢			
Pyrethrum	🔵	🔵				🔵	🟢🟢	🟢	🟢	🟢		
Rudbeckia	🟢🟢	🟢🟢	🟢🟢	🟢					🟡	🟡	🟡	🟡🟡
Salpiglossis	🟢🟢	🟢🟢	🟢🟢	🟢	🟡	🟡	🟡	🟡	🟡	🟡		🟢
Salvia	🟡🟢🟢	🟢🟢🟢	🟢🟢🟢	🟢🟢🟢	🟡	🟡	🟡	🟡	🟡	🟡	🟡	🟢🟢
Schizanthus					🟢🟢	🟢🟢	🟡🟢🟢	🟢🟢🟢	🟢🟢	🟢		
Snapdragon	🟡🟢🟢	🟢🟢🟢	🟢🟢🟢	🟢🟢	🟢🟢	🟢🟢	🟢🟢	🟢🟢	🟢🟢	🟡	🟡	🟢🔵
Statice	🟢🟢	🔵				🟢	🟢🟢🟢	🟢🟢🟢	🟢🟢🟢	🟢🟢	🟢🟢	🟢
Stock					🟢🟢	🟢🟢🟢	🟢🟢🟢	🟢🟢🟢	🟢			
Sunflower	🟡🟢🟢	🟢🟢🟢	🟢🟢🟢	🟢🟢🟢	🟡	🟡	🟡	🟡	🟡			🟡🟡
Swan River daisy	🟢🟢	🟢🟢	🟢🟢	🟢🟢					🟡	🟡	🟡	🟡🟡
Sweet pea	🔵	🔵				🟢🟢	🟡🟢🟢	🟢🟢	🟢🟢			
Sweet William	🟡🟢🟢	🟢🟢	🟢			🔵	🟡🟢🟢	🟢🟢	🟢🟢	🟡🟡	🟡🟡	🟡🟡
Thunbergia	🟡🟢🟢	🟢🟢	🟢				🟡	🟡	🟡			🟡🟡
Torenia	🟡🟢🟢	🟢🟢🟢	🟢🟢🟢	🟢🟢🟢			🟡	🟡	🟡			🟡🟡
Verbena	🟡🟢🟢	🟢🟢	🟢🟢	🟢🟢	🟢🟢	🟢🟢	🟡	🟡		🟡		🟡🟡
Vinca	🟡🟢🟢	🟢🟢🟢	🟢🟢	🟡🟢🟢	🟢🟢🟢	🟢🟢🟢	🟢🟢🟢	🟢				🟡
Viola	🔵	🔵			🔵	🟢🟢	🟢🟢🟢	🟢🟢🟢	🟢🟢			
Virginian stock	🔵	🔵				🟢🟢	🟡🟢🟢	🟢🟢🟢	🟢🟢			
Viscaria	🟢🟢	🟢🟢	🟢🟢	🟢🟢					🟡	🟡	🟡	🟡🟡
Wallflower					🟢🟢	🟢🟢	🟡🟢🟢	🟢🟢🟢	🟢🟢			
Zinnia	🟡🟢🟢	🟢🟢🟢	🟢🟢	🟢🟢🟢	🟡	🟡	🟡	🟡	🟡	🟡	🟡	🟡🟡
HERBS												
Basil	🟡🟢	🟡🟢🟢	🟢🟢🟢	🟡🟢🟢	🟢🟢	🟡	🟡	🟡	🟡	🟡	🟡	🟡
Borage	🟢🟢	🟡🟢🟢	🟢🟢	🔵			🟢	🟢	🟢			🟡
Chervil	🟢🟢	🟡🟢🟢	🟢🟢🟢	🟢🟢	🟢🟢	🟢				🟡	🟡	🟡
Chives; garlic chives	🟢🟢	🟡🟢🟢	🟢🟢🟢	🟢🟢🟢	🟢🟢🟢	🟢🟢🟢	🟢🟢	🟢	🟡	🟡	🟡	🟡
Coriander	🟡🟢	🟡🟢🟢	🟢🟢🟢	🟢🟢🟢	🟢🟢🟢	🟢🟢🟢	🟡🔵	🟢🟢	🟡	🟡	🟡	🟡
Dill	🟡🟢	🟡🟢🟢	🟢🟢🟢	🟢🟢🟢	🟢🟢🟢	🟢🟢🟢	🟢🟢	🟡	🟡	🟡	🟡	🟡
Lemon balm	🟡🟢🟢	🟢🟢🟢	🟢🟢🟢	🟢🟢	🟢🟢	🟢🟢	🟢🟢	🟡	🟡	🟡	🟡	
Marjoram	🟡🟢🟢	🟢🟢🟢	🟢🟢🟢	🟢🟢🟢	🟢🟢	🟢🟢	🟡🟢	🟢🟢	🟡	🟡		🟡🟡
Mint	🟡🟢🟢	🟢🟢🟢	🟢🟢🟢	🟢🟢	🟢🟢🟢	🟢🟢	🟢🟢	🟢🟢	🟢🟢	🟡	🟡	🟡
Oregano	🟡🟢🟢	🟡🟢🟢	🟢🟢🟢	🟢			🟢🟢	🟢🟢	🟢🟢	🟡	🟡	🟡

PLANT	SPRING			SUMMER			AUTUMN			WINTER		
	EARLY	MID	LATE	EARLY	MID	LATE	EARLY	MID	LATE	EARLY	MID	LATE
Parsley	●●	●●●	●●●	●●●	●●●	●●●	●●	●	●	●	●	●
Rosemary	●●	●●●	●●●	●●			●	●	●	●	●	●
Sage	●	●●	●●	●●	●●	●●	●	●				
Thyme	●	●●	●●	●●	●●	●	●	●				
VEGETABLES												
Artichoke	●●	●●	●●	●				●●	●●	●●	●●	●
Bean	●●	●●●	●●●	●●	●	●●	●	●	●	●	●	●
Broad bean	●						●	●●●	●●	●●	●	●
Beetroot	●●●	●●●		●●	●●	●●●	●	●	●		●●	●●
Broccoli			●	●●	●●	●●	●●	●●	●	●	●	●
Cabbage	●●●	●●●	●●●	●●●	●●	●●	●	●	●	●	●	●●●
Capsicum;chilli	●●●	●●●	●●●	●●	●	●	●	●	●	●	●	●●●
Carrot	●●●	●●●	●●●	●●	●●	●●●	●●	●	●		●●	●●●
Cauliflower			●	●	●●	●●	●●	●●	●			
Celery	●●	●●	●●	●●	●●	●●	●	●				
Chicory	●●●	●●	●●	●●	●●	●●	●●●	●	●	●	●	●●
Chinese cabbage	●●●	●●●	●●●	●●●	●●●	●●●	●●●	●	●	●	●●	●●●
Chinese mustard	●	●●●	●●●	●●●	●●●	●●●	●●●	●	●●	●	●	●
Chopsuey greens	●●●	●●●	●●●				●●	●●	●●	●●	●	●●●
Cress	●●●	●●●	●●●	●●●	●●●	●●●	●●●	●●●	●●●	●●●	●●●	●●●
Cucumber	●●	●●●	●●●	●●●	●●	●	●	●	●	●	●	●
Eggplant	●●	●●●	●●●	●●	●	●	●	●	●	●	●	●
Endive	●●	●●	●●	●●	●●	●●	●●	●	●	●	●	●●
Kale	●●●	●●	●●	●●	●●	●●	●●	●●●	●●●	●●●	●	●
Kohlrabi	●●	●			●●	●●●	●●●	●	●			●
Lamb's lettuce	●●	●●	●●	●●	●●	●●	●					
Leek	●	●●	●●	●●	●●	●●	●●●	●	●	●		
Lettuce	●●●	●●●	●●●	●●●	●●●	●●●	●●●	●●●	●●●	●●●	●●●	●●●
Marrow	●●	●●●	●●●	●●●	●●	●	●	●	●	●	●	●
Melon	●●	●●●	●●●	●●●	●	●	●	●	●	●	●	●
Mustard	●●●	●●●	●●●	●●●	●●●	●●●	●●●	●●●	●●●	●●●	●●●	●●●
Okra	●●	●●●	●●●	●●●	●		●	●	●	●	●	●
Onion; shallot	●					●	●●	●●●	●●●	●●	●●	●
Pak choi	●●●	●●●	●●●	●●●	●●●	●●●	●●●	●●	●	●	●●	●●●
Parsnip	●●●	●●	●●	●●	●●	●●●	●●	●	●	●	●●	●●
Pea	●	●				●●	●●	●●	●●	●●●	●●●	●
Potato tubers	●●●	●	●	●	●	●●	●	●	●	●	●●	●●●
Pumpkin	●●	●●●	●●●	●●●	●	●	●	●	●	●	●	●
Radicchio	●●	●	●				●	●●	●●	●●	●●	●●●
Radish	●●	●●●	●●●	●●●	●●●	●●●	●●●	●●●	●●	●	●	●●
Rocket	●●●	●●●	●●●	●●●	●●●	●●●	●●●	●●●	●●●	●●●	●●	●●
Salsify	●●	●●	●●	●●	●●	●	●●	●	●	●	●●	●●
Silver beet	●●●	●●●	●●●	●●●	●●	●●	●	●	●	●	●●	●●●
Spinach						●●	●●	●●●	●●●	●●●	●●	●
Spring onion	●●●	●●●	●●●	●●●	●●●	●●●	●●●	●●●	●●	●	●	●●●
Squash	●●	●●●	●●●	●●●	●	●	●	●	●	●	●	●
Swede	●				●●	●●●	●●	●				●
Sweet corn	●●	●●●	●●●	●●●	●	●	●	●	●	●	●	●●
Tomato	●●●	●●●	●●●	●●	●	●	●	●	●	●	●	●●
Turnip	●	●			●●	●●●	●●●	●●			●	●
Zucchini	●●	●●●	●●●	●●●	●●	●	●	●	●	●	●	●

*This chart gives possible sowing times. See the text for the optimum sowing season.

Index

Published by Murdoch Books®, a subsidiary of Murdoch Magazines Pty Ltd,
GPO Box 1203, Sydney NSW 1045

Commissioning Editor, Gardening: Diana Hill
Editors: Christine Eslick, Diana Hill
Designer: Wing Ping Tong
Consultant for Mr. Fothergill's Seeds Pty Ltd: Phil Tapping
Text Consultant: Tim Yates
Stylist (back cover, page 112): Sophie Ward
Illustrator: Willo Studio (Sonya Naumov)
Cartoonist: Greg Gaul Graphics

General Manager: Mark Smith
CEO & Publisher: Anne Wilson

National Library of Australia Cataloguing-in-Publication Data
Hanks, Margaret. Growing from Seed
Includes index. ISBN 0 86411 946 1.
1. Seeds. 2. Plant propagation. 3. Gardening.
I. Title. 635.0421

Photographs: Courtesy of Floramedia/Macbird Floraprint (copyright reserved) (all
unless otherwise specified); Dell Adam (86L); The Digger's Club (122 aboveL & 128
topL, 150 upperR); George Mourtzakis (back cover, 112); Mr. Fothergill's Seeds Ltd
(38 topL & aboveL, 45 top & above, 46 topL, topR & aboveL, 48 aboveR, 51L & R, 55
centre & R, 62 centre, 63 topL, 65 aboveL, 67 top, 68 bottomR, 72 aboveR, 75 topR &
centreL, 80R, 81 top centre, topR & aboveL, 83 top, 84 topL, 85 aboveL, 88 aboveL,
topR & aboveR, 93 top, 94 all, 96 topL, 96 upperL & upperR, 96 lowerL & lower centre,
96 aboveL, above centre & aboveR, 106 topR, 107 all, 108 all, 109 all, 110 bottomR,
111 all, 120 topL, 121 topL & above centre, 122 above centre, 124 topR, aboveL &
above centre, 127L & centre, 131R, 139L, 142 above centre, 146 topR, 150 top centre,
152 topL); Murdoch Books® Picture Library (32, 102, 112).

The publisher thanks the University of New South Wales Ecoliving Centre and
Permaculture Community Garden, 14 Arthur St, Randwick NSW 2031 (phone (02)
9316 9199; email sswb@mpx.com.au). The public is welcome to visit the Garden and
participate in its volunteer program and training courses.

Produced by Phoenix Offset
PRINTED IN CHINA